Introducing
Catholic Prayer
for RCIA Leaders

A COMPANION TO
THE CATHOLIC WAY TO PRAY

KATHLEEN GLAVICH, SND

INTRODUCING CATHOLIC PRAYER FOR RCIA LEADERS

A Companion to *The Catholic Way to Pray*

TWENTY THIRD 23rd
PUBLICATIONS
www.23rdpublications.com

TWENTY-THIRD PUBLICATIONS
A Division of Bayard
One Montauk Avenue, Suite 200
New London, CT 06320
(860) 437-3012 or (800) 321-0411
www.23rdpublications.com

Cover image: ©iStockphoto.com/creativeeye99

The Scripture passages contained herein are from the *New Revised
Standard Version of the Bible*, copyright ©1989, by the Division of
Christian Education of the National Council of Churches in the
U.S.A. All rights reserved.

ISBN 978-1-58595-756-9
Library of Congress Catalog Card Number: 2009926152
Printed in the U.S.A.

Contents

Introduction

As you accompany the catechumens and candidates on their spiritual journey, one of your main tasks will be to guide them in prayer. Some of them may already enjoy a vibrant prayer life that nourishes their relationship with God. These experts, though, may not be familiar with the variety of prayer methods available to them. For some of your catechumens, praying may be a totally new experience, one that is mystifying as well as intimidating. Chances are, all of your catechumens will be strangers to most traditional Catholic prayers.

Your catechumenate probably includes one or two sessions devoted to the topic of prayer. This book is a resource that can help you present prayer to your group in an interesting and appealing way. It contains the fundamental concepts of prayer, giving you the background to explain prayer and field questions about it. In addition, the book provides an overview of the many types of prayers and prayer methods, a feature that may expand your own prayer repertoire! What you may find most useful are the anecdotes marked "Story," the numerous "Tips," as well as the "Activities" geared to help your catechumens understand

and practice prayer. Moreover, interspersed throughout the chapters are questions about prayer that catechumens typically ask, along with possible answers.

If you invite guest speakers or a panel to cover your sessions on prayer, you might give them a copy of this book. They can draw on the information in it to embellish their presentations. Over and above the structured sessions on prayer, you will want to integrate prayer throughout your process. You'll find a trove of ideas for doing so in this book.

Notice that the Appendix contains examples and material that you are free to duplicate as you develop the concepts about prayer. The book concludes with a glossary of Catholic prayer words as an easy reference for you.

The adage "You can't give what you haven't got" applies to teaching prayer. If you yourself are a person of prayer, your words will ring true and enkindle in your listeners a desire to pray. As you share the rich prayer traditions of the Catholic Church with your catechumens, may you too grow in your knowledge of prayer life, but more important, may you find that prayer becomes for you as simple and as essential as breathing.

A note on language: As a pure spirit, God has no gender, and both masculine and feminine images for God can enrich prayer. However, it's been a long-standing tradition to use masculine pronouns for God, and they occur in our liturgy and prayers. So far, attempts to address this discrepancy in our language have been awkward and unsatisfactory. In this book, then, you will find masculine pronouns for God.

TIP Keep a list of the names of your catechumens and candidates where you will see it and remember to pray for them.

1

Preparing to Teach Prayer

One woman wrote to a Catholic magazine, "It is not so much that I do not want to pray or can't pray—it is that I really do not know how to pray. I think I would do more if I felt comfortable doing it." Some of the people in your catechumenate this year might wholeheartedly echo her words. They and others in the group look to you and request what the apostles asked Jesus, "Teach us to pray." You have the awesome and privileged task of leading them into the ways of prayer, a vital component of their formation as Catholics. Following are some surefire steps to create a solid base of prayer in your catechumens and candidates.

This Book

Read this book and determine how to adapt it to your program. What concepts will you include in your sessions? Which activities? What prayer methods will you teach? When in your calendar will you allocate the material? Meeting your catechumens and getting to know them will help you answer these questions so as to best serve their needs.

A Prayerful Team

Plan how you and the other members on the RCIA team can become a powerhouse of prayer yourselves. Consider these ideas:

- Start off the program with a retreat just for the team members and focus it on your ministry as RCIA leaders. Include prayer, a speaker, and songs.

- Gather as a team before and after sessions to pray together briefly, especially for your catechumens.

- Agree to spend a few moments of prayer for blessings on the program during the day of the sessions, maybe even at the same hour.

Presenters

Brainstorm with your team to decide on speakers to present the sessions on prayer. Possibilities include you, a team member, a parish priest, another parishioner, or an outside expert. You might line up several speakers or organize a panel. Be specific on what you wish the speakers to present. (For example, what prayer means to them, when and how they pray, and how their prayer habits have changed.) Encourage your catechumens to have questions for the speakers ready.

The Setting

Arrange and decorate the room where you meet so that it is conducive to prayer. Make it pleasant and neat, beautify it with flowers and plants, and display religious items, statues, pictures, and posters. Light a candle or use incense (if no one is allergic to it).

Prayer Materials

Build a collection of materials that will aid in teaching about prayer. You might be able to share resources, such as a set of DVDs on the psalms, with a nearby parish. Your collection could include the following items:

- an assortment of prayer books
- rosaries
- Bibles
- CDs or tapes of music for prayer
- candles
- incense
- Stations of the Cross booklets
- prayer services
- a labyrinth
- posters about prayer
- audiovisuals that teach about prayer

Prayer Quotations

Decorate handouts for all your sessions with quotations about prayer:

"A life hemmed by prayer is less likely to unravel."

"If you are too busy to pray, you are too busy."

"Seven days without prayer makes one weak."

"Let your knees take some of the strain off your heart."

"Courage is fear that has said its prayers."

"Prayer changes people and people change the times."

"More things are wrought by prayer than this world dreams of." (Alfred Lord Tennyson)

"In prayer it is better to have a heart without words than words without a heart." (John Bunyan)

"You need to speak to Jesus less with your lips than with your heart." (Saint [Padre] Pio de Pietrelcina)

Prayer Humor

Spice up your sessions by interjecting prayer jokes related to your topic. You might receive some via your e-mail. In teaching about petitions for example, tell the anecdote of the little boy who prays, "Thank you for my new baby sister, God, but it was a puppy I asked for."

TIP   *If with permission you record or videotape someone who speaks on prayer, you will have a ready-made presentation for the following year. Live people are much better, but the tape might come in handy.*

The Parish Community

Involve the whole parish in praying for the catechumens by posting their names and pictures in church and in the church bulletin. Remind parishioners to pray for the catechumens at the different stages of their journey.

STORY: *THREE HERMITS*

Keep in mind that your catechumens come with their
own experiences with prayer. Decide how you can
draw on this personal resource during your sessions.
"The Three Hermits," a Russian folktale told by Leo
Tolstoy, holds a good message for us teachers of
prayer. Here is a condensed version:

A bishop was traveling by boat. As it passed an
island, someone explained that three very old
hermits with long beards lived there. The hermits
communicated only with a glance. The bishop
asked the captain to take him to the island, but
the captain replied, "They are only foolish fellows
who say no more than the fish of the sea."

Nevertheless, the captain had the bishop
rowed to shore, where the bishop met the three
hermits standing hand-in-hand. He told them that
he was called to teach Christ's flock and wanted to
teach them too.

"How do you pray?" he asked.

The three hermits then chanted, "Three are ye,
three are we, have mercy upon us."

"You have heard something of the Trinity," said
the bishop, "but you do not pray right. This is how
the Savior taught us to pray. Repeat after me: Our
Father."

The three repeated, "Our Father."

The bishop said, "Who art in heaven." He
stayed all day, teaching each line of the prayer,
sometimes saying a word a hundred times.

When the moon appeared, the bishop rose
to return to the ship. The hermits bowed low to
him. As the bishop was rowed back to the ship, he
could hear the hermits repeating the Lord's Prayer.

After dark, the bishop sat in the stern thinking how pleased the good old men were to learn the Lord's Prayer. He thanked God for sending him to teach them. Suddenly he saw something white and shining across the sea coming closer and closer. He realized that it was the three hermits. They were gliding upon the water all gleaming white and approaching the ship as quickly as though it were not moving.

The steersman yelled, "O Lord, they're running on the water as if it were dry land!"

The hermits overtook the boat and addressed the bishop: "We have forgotten your teaching. First a word dropped out, and then another, and now it has all gone to pieces. Teach us again."

The bishop leaned over the ship's side and said, "Your own prayer will reach the Lord. Pray for us sinners," and he bowed low before the old men. They turned and went back across the sea. All that night a bright light shone where they were lost to sight.

2

What *Prayer* Is

A little girl once confided to her teacher, "Sometimes I think of God even when I'm not praying." The child didn't know that she was praying according to the time-honored definition of prayer found in the *Catechism of the Catholic Church*: "the raising of the mind and heart to God." Any time we reflect on God, respond to God with mind or heart, or are in communion with God, we are at prayer. It's been said that most people pray more and better than they think they do.

Why We Pray

Every one of us has been created by God and is destined to live with him forever. We were made for union with our Triune God. Jane Ubertino sums up why we pray by saying. "We pray because God is God and we are we, and therefore that meeting is the most important thing in our life."

God loved us first and desires to be with us. He haunts us. As C.S. Lewis noted, "People seeking God is like a mouse seeking a cat." On the other hand, we have a strong desire to be with God, our good and loving Creator. We hunger for what is true, good, and beautiful; and God is absolute truth, goodness, and beauty. St. Augustine expressed this innate human desire when he declared to God, "Our hearts are restless until they rest in you." Our God-ache is compared to having a hole in our heart that only God can fill. Philosopher Blaise Pascal called it a God-shaped vacuum. That's why we experience a kind of gravitational pull toward God. St. Catherine of Siena nicely describes what happens during prayer when she said to God, "You are a mystery as deep as the sea. The more I search, the more I find, and the more I find, the more I search for you. But I can never be satisfied; what I receive will ever leave me desiring more. When you fill my soul, I have an even greater hunger, and I grow more famished for your light."

God invites us to enter into a relationship of love with him. In human love relationships communication is key. The same is true in fostering a personal relationship with God. Communication with God, both listening and speaking to him, is prayer. It is as necessary to our spiritual life as breathing is to our physical life. God doesn't need our prayer, but we do. Knowing that God exists makes sense out of the universe. Praying to him gives meaning to our lives.

Fortunately communication with God can be instant. First of all, God is everywhere and on call 24/7. Put mathematically, God is a circle whose center is everywhere and whose circumference is nowhere. God knows our very thoughts and sees our every action. As St. Paul preached, "In him we live and move and have our being" (Acts 17:28). In addition, there is the mystery of the divine indwelling, that is, God dwells within our very being. He tugs at our hearts for attention. At any time we can sink down into the cave of our hearts for an encounter with God.

STORY: *THE LITTLE FISH*

One day a little fish swam up to an older fish and asked, "Where is the thing called ocean?" The older fish answered, "It's what you're swimming in." "But this is just water," countered the little fish, and he swam away, continuing to search for the ocean. In the same way, we are surrounded by God but don't always realize it or accept it.

Another reason to pray is that prayer makes us better persons. Through prayer we receive graces that help us to live the Gospel values and grow in virtues like faith, hope, and charity. In addition, prayer is a means for removing temporal punishment due for sins, that is, the punishment that helps make up for our forgiven sins either on earth or in purgatory.

Beyond this practical reason to pray is the fact that prayer is life's most intoxicating high, the peak experience. In prayer we find satisfaction, fulfillment, and peace. But perhaps the most convincing argument for prayer is that there is something far greater than our desire to pray, namely, God's desire that we pray.

To motivate your catechumens to pray, offer examples of how important prayer was and is to certain people. Here are some examples:

- Abraham Lincoln once explained, "I have been driven many times to my knees by the overwhelming conviction that I had nowhere else to go. My wisdom and that of all round me seemed insufficient for the day."

STORY: *CARDINAL JOSEPH BERNARDIN*

Cardinal Bernardin of Chicago, Illinois, was a very busy man. His fellow priests were concerned about him and advised that he take time to pray. The cardinal acted on their advice and began rising an hour earlier in order to pray. With prayer as a prelude, his days went much smoother. In fact, Cardinal Bernardin had to face two crises: He was falsely accused of sexual impropriety, and he was diagnosed with pancreatic cancer. His strong prayer life gave Cardinal Bernardin the stamina to meet these crises with grace.

- St. Rose Philippine Duchesne used to pray for so long that the Native Americans called her "the woman who always prays." There is a story that one day a young Indian lad set some corn seeds on St. Rose's skirts while she prayed. When he returned a long time later, the seeds were still just as he had placed them.

?

How do you explain that some people who don't believe in God and never pray are still good people?

They are good by the grace of God. Imagine how much richer and more Christlike their lives would be if they prayed.

- George Washington Carver is famous for making some 300 products from the peanut. A man of prayer, he credited God for his success, explaining that he arose each morning at four o'clock and walked in the woods. He asserted, "In the woods, while most other persons are sleeping, I hear and understand God's plan for me."

 Impress on your catechumens that the best way to learn to pray is by praying.

Praying to the Trinity

In praying to God we are praying to all three persons of the Trinity. Most people, however, focus on the Father or Jesus. Therefore the Holy Spirit has been called the Cinderella of the Trinity. Truly Christian prayer is directed to the Father, the Son, and the Holy Spirit.

Ways to Pray

Prayer comes in many varieties. It would be good to begin and end each session with a different kind of prayer. The catechumens will be more likely to adopt a prayer style once they have experienced it. In this book are chapters that explain several prayer methods in depth. Cover as many as possible because different people have different prayer preferences. Moreover, these preferences change over time. Teach your catechumens the many options for prayer, and you will be preparing them for their future needs. Here is a listing of prayer styles:

- Vocal (said aloud) prayer or mental (thought) prayer
- Personal (private) prayer or group (communal) prayer
- Traditional formulas, such as the Our Father and Hail Mary, some of which have a long history

- Prayers composed by saints and other people. Sometimes these express for us the exact thoughts and feelings we have in our hearts.

- Our original written compositions

- Spontaneous (informal) prayer

- Singing or listening to a hymn. Many hymns are Scripture verses with musical settings.

- Meditation, that is, thinking about God. We can meditate on Scripture passages, prayer books, pictures, or our own experiences.

- Affective prayer, which is responding to God with various sentiments, such as love and adoration

- Contemplation, the highest form of prayer, a wordless prayer in which we simply rest quietly in God's presence. We bask in God's love. Intuition more than reasoning is involved here. The word *contemplation* comes from the Latin *con*, which means "with" and the word for "temple." To contemplate is to be with God in a sacred place, in the temple. St. John of the Cross called contemplation "silent love."

TIP *Always invite, never force, people to pray "spontaneous" prayer. The same thing holds for having them share what they have experienced in prayer.*

The progression of prayer from vocal to contemplative is comparable to the stages of communication between two people in a love relationship. At first the two talk a lot: face-to-face, on the phone, by e-mail, or text messaging. They wish to learn as much as possible about each other and simultaneously to reveal information, even secrets, about themselves to the other. As the relationship deepens, talking is not that necessary. The couple can read each other's minds and communicate just by a glance. After much time together, two people in love are content simply to be in each other's presence wordlessly. Similarly prayer parallels the stages of intimacy: knowledge, communication, surrender, and, ultimately, union. In the words of the thirteenth-century mystic Juliana of Norwich, "Prayer one-eth the soul to God."

Stages of Prayer

St. Teresa of Avila was named a Doctor of the Church in 1970 and given the title "Teacher of Prayer." She defined prayer as "a conversation with one who you know loves you." St. Teresa uses four methods of watering a garden as an analogy for the stages of prayer.

1. The first method is to draw water from a well with a bucket attached to a rope. This is parallel to the first stage of prayer, vocal prayer and discursive meditation. We are active, exercising our bodies and minds.

2. The second method of watering is using a waterwheel by which water is poured into a trough that carries it to the garden. In this stage the person is recollected and enjoying contentment.

3. The third method of watering is irrigating by means of a running stream. This is like the stage of prayer that involves no human effort. It is a mystical prayer in which the soul is united with God. The faculties

are so totally absorbed in God that they are quieted or "asleep."

4. The final method for watering a garden is by rain. The comparable stage of prayer is infused by God and called prayer of union.

Mysticism

Mysticism is the direct experience of God enjoyed in the last two stages of prayer.

These two stages are not the result of our actions but are God's doing. Some saints have enjoyed these types of prayer. St. Teresa, who experienced the extreme joy of union with God called rapture, describes these extraordinary stages of prayer in her writings. In case someone in your group asks about them, here is an overview:

Infused recollection: This is the first degree of infused, mystical contemplation.

Prayer of quiet: The will is totally captivated by divine love. Sometimes all the faculties are likewise captivated, resulting in ecstasy, a state in which the senses of the person are halted and he or she appears asleep or even lifeless.

Prayer of simple union: The intellect and the will are absorbed in God.

Prayer of ecstatic union: This is called the "mystical espousal" or "conforming union."

Prayer of transforming union: This highest stage is called the "mystical marriage" because it is the most intimate union of the soul with God that is possible in this life.

In passing from one stage of prayer to another, people may experience what is called the night of the senses, or the dark night of the soul. This is a state marked by aridity in prayer, confused ideas about God, and sadness. The letters of Blessed Mother Teresa of Calcutta reveal that she was in this painful state where she didn't experience the presence of God for about fifty years.

Point out that the goal of prayer is not preternatural gifts, such as ecstasy, levitation (rising above the ground), and bilocation (being in two places at once). Our goal is higher than those phenomena, namely, to be united with God. This is not a destiny confined to great saints, but is meant for everyone. Theologian Karl Rahner said, "In the coming age we must all become mystics—or be nothing at all."

STORY: CONTEMPLATION

St. John Vianney, also known as the Curé of Ars, noticed a man sitting quietly for hours every day in his parish church. One day the priest asked the man what he was doing. The man replied, "I look at him and he looks at me."

Informal Prayer

The easiest way to pray is to talk to God about whatever is on our minds. This is usually just the stuff of daily life. In the evening we can imagine God asking, "So, how was your day?" In heart-to-heart talks, we share with God our fears, desires, passions, dreams, disappointments, worries, joys, and sorrows. We are forthright with God, knowing that we will never shock him and that his love for us in uncondi-tional. The Carmelite nun St. Thérèse of Lisieux, known

?

What is praying in tongues?

People who have undergone what is known as baptism of the Holy Spirit pray spontaneously with great joy in words that are unrecognizable. This prayer, the gift of tongues, is a charismatic gift. Some people have a different charismatic gift that enables them to interpret what is being said. St. Paul could speak in tongues, but he teaches, "In church I would rather speak five words with my mind, in order to instruct others also, than ten thousand words in a tongue" (1 Corinthians 14:19).

for her "little way," admitted, "I have not the courage to search through books for beautiful prayers....Unable either to say them all or choose between them, I do as a child would do who cannot read—I say just what I want to say to God, quite simply, and He never fails to understand." This informal, familiar conversation proves to be a very effective form of prayer: Thérèse died at age twenty-four and became a saint.

Talking to God is only one side of the coin. When Blessed Mother Teresa of Calcutta was asked, "When you pray, what do you say to God?" she answered, "I listen." St. Benedict recommends listening "with the ears of our heart."

TIP *You might prime the pump and lead the catechumens into prayer with "starters," such as quotations from books, open-ended statements, and questions.*

ACTIVITIES

1. To introduce the topic of prayer, distribute a list of definitions of prayer and have the catechumens choose the one they like best and tell why.

   → See #1 on page 188 for a list of definitions.

2. Form groups of three and have the members talk about their favorite way to pray.

3. Use comic strips about prayer as a springboard for discussion. These appear more often than you may think. Start collecting these comic strips and laminate them.

4. Read aloud Psalm 139:1–18 to reinforce the concept that God is always near.

5. Bring to the session articles clipped from newspapers and magazines that show prayer playing a role in people's lives.

3

Prayer Forms

Y ou might have been taught the acronym ACTS as a way to remember the four forms of prayer (Adoration, Contrition, Thanksgiving, and Supplication). Now the *Catechism of the Catholic Church* identifies five basic forms of prayer that are found in Scripture and the liturgies of the first Christians. Some prayers are a combination of one or more of these forms. The five forms are explained below and an example of each is provided.

1. Blessing/Adoration

God blesses us, that is, gives us good gifts. In return we bless, or adore, God, which means we acknowledge and celebrate God's greatness and goodness. Adoration is the primary stance of human beings before God, who is our creator, our savior, and the master of the universe. God is the unnamable one, the utterly Other, a profound mystery whom we will never understand and on whom we are totally dependent. Who can gaze at the ocean, a sunset, or a newborn baby and not respond with awe and adoration for God? As the poet Wordsworth wrote, "My heart leaps up when I behold a rainbow in the sky." Fr. Edward Hays muses that the oldest and shortest of all prayers was an expression of awe at the wonders of God's world. When our early ancestors saw green shoots breaking through earth from seed, when they saw a rainbow, a sunrise, or a night sky spangled with stars, they responded, "Ohhh!" Although worship is a natural response to our almighty and all-loving God, the first commandment obliges us to worship.

Clarify for the catechumens that Catholics adore God alone. This adoration of the divine is called *latria*. We do

?

What does it mean when Catholics receive a blessing or have their houses, rosaries, and medals blessed?

A blessing is a sacramental that asks God's favor, assistance, and grace upon a person or object. (A sacramental is a sacred sign through which grace is given by the merits of Jesus and prayers of the Church and dependent on the faith of the recipient.) A blessing is usually imparted by an ordained minister but can also be given by a lay person. In a blessing, words may be accompanied by outstretched hands, the laying on of hands, the Sign of the Cross, or the sprinkling of holy water. Throats are blessed for protection on the feast of St. Blaise, and animals are blessed on the feast of St. Francis of Assisi. The United States bishops have published the book **Catholic Household Blessings and Prayers**. *It contains blessings for different occasions, such as on bringing a child into the home, in times of trouble, and on anniversaries. One woman who must fly often traces a cross on the outside of the plane each time she departs.*

not adore the Blessed Virgin Mary and the other saints who, though holy, are still merely human beings. The honor or veneration we give to the saints is called *dulia*; the honor we give to Mary, the Mother of God, is called *hyperdulia*.

Example: See the Divine Praises on page 141.

> **TIP** Suggest to the catechumens that they bless their children and spouses each night. Tell them that when we receive a blessing we make the Sign of the Cross over ourselves.

2. Petition

Someone quipped, "As long as there are tests, there will be prayers in public schools." We depend on God for everything, not just for help in tests. Jesus always answered when people asked him for help. What's more, he advised us to ask the Father in his name for what we need. The main thing we stand in need of is forgiveness. Therefore, we express our contrition and petition the Father to forgive us. We also ask God that his kingdom of peace and justice come. We can request God to give us anything else for ourselves, even things we might consider trivial, confident that he will hear us. A prayer of petition is an act of faith.

Example: The "Lord, have mercy" at Mass

3. Intercession

All the members of the Church are interdependent. When others are in need, we turn trustingly to our good God with prayers of supplication for them. In this way we imitate Jesus, who is constantly interceding for us. Scripture assures us that we can help one another by our prayers: "I urge that supplications, prayers, intercessions, and thanksgivings be made for everyone, for kings and all who are in high positions, so that we may lead a quiet and peaceable life in all godliness and dignity. This is good, and pleases God our Savior" (1 Timothy 2:1–3).

We Catholics believe in praying for the deceased. If they are in purgatory, our prayers will hasten their purification process. We have the custom of sending the grieving family a Mass card informing them that we have had a Mass said for the repose of the soul of their loved one. At our request and for a donation some religious congregations will have a Mass said and provide a Mass card. We can also have a Mass offered for the deceased at a parish.

A *spiritual bouquet* is a gift of prayers and good deeds offered for the recipient and his or her intentions. We list our promises in a card, for example, "I offer three Hail Marys, three Our Fathers, and three acts of charity." These gifts can be creative, such as "five extra minutes of prayer each day for a week," "working two days in a soup kitchen," or "attending a Saturday morning Mass."

Example: The Prayers of the Faithful at Mass

STORY: A SAINTLY INTERCESSOR

When St. Thérèse of Lisieux was a young girl, a murderer named Pranzini was to be guillotined. Unrepentant, he refused to see a priest. Thérèse prayed and sacrificed for Pranzini's conversion and asked for a sign to let her know if he was saved. Newspapers reported that even on the scaffold Pranzini showed no remorse. Then at the last minute when the executioner's assistant held him by the hair, Pranzini asked for a crucifix and kissed it three times. Later as a Carmelite nun Thérèse had Masses said for Pranzini.

TIP *Encourage the catechumens to visualize the people or situations they are praying for. A vivid picture in their minds will intensify their prayer.*

4. Thanksgiving

When we receive gifts, graces, and favors, it's only common courtesy to express our gratitude to God with prayers of thanksgiving. Jesus shows that he values this form of prayer when he expresses disappointment that out of ten cured lepers only one is thoughtful enough to thank him. Meister Eckhart, a mystic, commented, "If the only prayer you say in your entire life is thank you, it will be enough."

Example: The Eucharist is our greatest expression of thanks.

TIP *Point out that we can express gratitude in times of trial. For example, when I have a car accident I can thank God that I have a car; and when I need to take medication I can thank God that I have health care.*

5. Praise

When someone exhibits an admirable quality or achieves something remarkable, our response is to acknowledge this with a compliment. Likewise, moved by God's power, goodness, or love, we praise him. Glorifying God because he is God is the chief occupation of the angels and saints in heaven. Incidentally, the word *alleluia* means "praise God." (*Hallel* is Hebrew for praise and *yah* is the first syllable of Yahweh, God's personal name.) And *Amen* means "I agree."

Example: Psalm 150

Love

Sometimes we are so taken with God and God's love and mercy that we pray prayers of sheer love. Edward Farrell wrote a book entitled *Prayer Is a Hunger*. This title is a good description of prayer. It is love, longing to be with God. In a real love relationship, neither person is concerned about getting something out of it. Each one desires not to receive, but to give. The same is true for our relationship with God. We spend time with God because we know it pleases him. And in prayer we let God love us.

Why do we ask God for things when he already knows what we need?

Apparently God wants us to articulate our needs. Before healing the blind man, for example, Jesus asked him, "What do you want me to do for you?" Jesus encouraged us to ask, to seek, and to knock. (See Matthew 7:7–11.)

Example: See the prayer of St. Francis Xavier on page 150.

Making an Intention

Catholics believe in the communion of saints, which means all saints in heaven, all souls in purgatory, and "all sorts" on earth bound together in the Body of Christ. One corollary of this doctrine is that the good performed by one or several members can be applied to others. We can "offer up" facets of our lives—our works, our prayers, our sacrifices, and our sufferings—for certain intentions and trust that God will apply them. For example, we can offer up a difficult project or a painful surgery for the intention of our mother who is ill or for peace in the Middle East. This Catholic practice infuses meaning into our everyday actions and in particular into our sufferings. When we encounter a disappointment or a trial, we can always "kiss it up to God," that is, offer it to God and put it to good use.

Periods of Prayer

Explain the following terms:

- An *octave* is eight days of prayer. Prayer for Christian Unity is an octave from January 18 to January 25 during which we pray that all Christians may be one. Christmas and the seven days after it are the Octave of Christmas.

- A *novena* is praying a certain prayer nine consecutive days or nine hours. Novenas began in imitation of the nine days that Mary and the disciples prayed while awaiting the coming of the Holy Spirit. People pray novenas to obtain a favor or to honor Jesus or a saint. A Christmas novena, for example, honors the nine months Jesus spent in Mary's womb. Here is the prayer that is prayed during the Exaltation of the Holy Cross Novena:

Jesus, who because of your burning love for us willed to be crucified and to shed your most precious blood for the redemption and salvation of our souls, look down upon us and grant the petition we ask for (mention here).

We trust completely in your mercy. Cleanse us from sin by your grace, sanctify our work, give us and all those who are dear to us our daily bread, lighten the burden of our sufferings, bless our families, and grant

to the nations, so sorely afflicted, your peace, which is
the only true peace, so that by obeying your command-
ments we may come at last to the glory of heaven.

- A **triduum** is three days of prayer that usually occurs before a special day. The three days from Holy Thursday evening to Easter Sunday evening are known as the Holy Triduum.

- A **retreat** is a period of prayer away from the busy-ness of ordinary life in which people concentrate on developing their relationship with God in silence and solitude. It is usually made under the guidance of a retreat director and can run from one to thirty days.

- A **day of recollection** is a retreat usually centered on a theme. It can last a day or part of a day.

Short Prayers

A centuries-old custom is the praying of one-line prayers called **aspirations** or ejaculations. These short prayers, or arrows shot to heaven, can be prayed throughout the day, lifting our minds and hearts to God in the midst of work. They are said to be like jewels added to our actions. (See #2 on page 189 for a collection of aspirations.)

Long Prayers

A **litany** is a rather long prayer invoking God or a saint under many titles. Each group of invocations is followed by the same response, such as "have mercy on us," or "pray for us." Most popular litanies are the Litany of Loreto to the Blessed Virgin Mary, the Litany of the Sacred Heart, the Litany of the Holy Spirit, and the Litany of Saints. (See the Litany of Loreto on page 134 and the Litany of the Holy Spirit on page 139.)

TIP *Before praying together, remind the group that Jesus promised that wherever two or three are gathered in his name, he is in their midst. Invite them to become aware of God's presence. They might imagine God looking at them with love.*

Prayer Styles

In addition to the various forms of prayer, some saints have taught different styles of prayer. No one way is better than the other. The variety can be explained through the image of light. Just as the spectrum of all colors is the result of a prism refracting light, all the styles of praying come from the one pure light of the Holy Spirit.

ACTIVITIES

1. Bless each catechumen as part of a prayer service or at the end of a session. This can be done by simply saying, "May God bless you." These or similar words can be accompanied by actions: raising your hand or hands over the catechumens, placing a Sign of the Cross on their foreheads or palms perhaps with holy oil, sprinkling them with holy water, or laying your hands on their heads. You can also invite the catechumens to bless one another.

2. Choose a prayer, such as the Our Father, a psalm, or a hymn and go through it line by line having the group determine what form or forms of prayer it exemplifies.

3. Arrange for the catechumens to have a prayer partner. Put their names in a box or bag and invite each person

to draw out a name. Explain to the catechumens that during the year they might pray in a special way for their prayer partner, asking God to bless him or her as they journey to their full commitment to Jesus.

4. Organize a prayer lab to introduce a variety of prayer methods. Set up stations around the room with materials and directions. Divide the catechumens into six groups and assign each a number. Have them go to the station with that number and follow the directions there. Every ten minutes or so, give the signal to have the groups move to the next station. Group six always moves to station one.

→ See #3 on page 190 for some sample activities for the prayer lab stations.

4

How God *Answers*

One *Dennis the Menace* cartoon shows Dennis ready to go upstairs to bed. He's asking his dad, "I'm going to pray now. Is there anything you want?" Most people's prayers are like Dennis's—prayers of petition or intercession. We need something, so we turn to God in hopes that he will give what we perceive we need.

But sometimes it seems that God doesn't hear our prayers. When this happens, it's a temptation to jump to these wrong conclusions: there is no God, I'm not a good pray-er, or even God doesn't love me. Instead, consider that God has several ways of answering. Sometimes God says yes, but other times God says no. Sometimes God answers in a way that we don't expect—or recognize. God may say, "Not yet," or "I have a better idea." Also, as former president Jimmy Carter pointed out, God may say, "Are you kidding?"

It's possible that what we ask of God works counter to his grand plan of salvation—even though what we ask appears good to us. Then our request cannot be fulfilled. In this case it helps to realize that through any difficulties or sufferings God will be at our side.

STORIES: *HOW GOD ANSWERS*

Archbishop Anthony Bloom illustrates in a striking way the advantage of God saying no: A young boy prayed that God would give him the gift his uncle had. Every night the uncle was able to remove his teeth and place them in a glass of water. When the boy grew up, he was very glad that God hadn't granted his prayer.

During a flood a man was trapped on his roof. A rowboat goes by but he refuses to get in, saying, "I'm praying to the Lord." A motorboat offers to rescue him and he says, "Go on. I'm praying to the Lord." A helicopter comes and he waves it on saying, "I'm praying to the Lord." In the end the man drowns. When he meets the Lord, he accuses, "I prayed to you. Why didn't you save me?" And God answers, "I sent you a rowboat, a motorboat, and a helicopter. What more did you want?"

A man lost in the desert and dying of thirst prays to be rescued. When he finally gets out of the desert, he tells someone how he prayed for help. "Did God help you?" his listener asks. "No," the man replies, "but an explorer came by and showed me the way out."

The Right Attitude

Jesus taught us the attitude to have before God when we desire something. During his agony in the garden, understandably Jesus asked the Father that the cup of suffering be taken away from him. But then he prayed, "Not my will but yours be done." Knowing that God is all-wise and loving, we trust him to do what is good, even if his plan doesn't make sense to us at the time. Like Mary, we leave ourselves totally open to God's will, confident that whatever God wants is really what we want.

Prayer is not mumbo-jumbo, words pronounced in order to bring about miracles in tight situations. Neither is prayer a way to have our will be done on earth. The goal of prayer is not to *change* God's mind but to *understand* God's mind. In prayer we seek to orient our whole self to God. The prayer of Dag Hammarskjöld expresses the right attitude about events in our life:

> *For all that has been—Thanks!*
> *For all that shall be—Yes!*

The prophet Habakkuk models faith for us in his beautiful prayer:

> *Though the fig tree does not blossom,*
>   *and no fruit is on the vines;*
> *though the produce of the oil fails*
>   *and the fields yield no food;*
> *though the flock is cut off from the fold*
>   *and there is no herd in the stalls,*
> *yet I will rejoice in the Lord;*
>   *I will exult in the God of my salvation.* Habakkuk 3:17–18

No Substitute for Work

Prayer doesn't mean that we don't have to work for what we want. Share this adage with your people: "Pray as though it all depended on God, but work as though it all depended on you."

Model prayer for the catechumens. When one of them has a special need, assure him or her, "I'll pray for you." Better still, pray for the person out loud on the spot. This can be an informal, spontaneous prayer or a formula prayer such as the Our Father. Having had the experience of being prayed for several times like this—even on the sidewalk and over the phone—I know how consoling and encouraging it can be.

Ways God Speaks

God communicates with us in several ways. First of all, in the words of Simone Weil, "The world is God's language to us." All of God's creation—mountains, trees, lakes, snow, flowers, dogs, our own marvelous bodies—shouts out his love for us and declares his power and glory. This is the point of poet Elizabeth Barrett Browning's words:

Earth's crammed with heaven,
And every common bush afire with God;
But only he who sees takes off his shoes,
The rest sit around and pluck blackberries.

In a special way God speaks to us in Sacred Scripture in which he reveals himself as our tremendous lover and savior. Sometimes God speaks to us through other people who come into our lives: family members, friends, or total strangers. Their words or example can carry a divine message for us. They can console us, encourage us, advise us, or warn us. And sometimes God says things to us through experiences we have, even our dreams. Most intimately God speaks to us through our own thoughts, either a progression of ideas or a sudden realization.

HOW GOD SPEAKS

The following reflection illustrates the wisdom of God's answers to prayer. It is attributed to an unknown Confederate soldier:

I asked for strength, that I might achieve;
I was made weak, that I might learn humbly to obey.

I asked for health, that I might do greater things;
I was given infirmity that I might do better things.

I asked for riches, that I might be happy;
I was given poverty, that I might be wise.
I asked for power, that I might have the praise of men;
I was given weakness, that I might feel the need for God.

I asked for all things, that I might enjoy life;
I was given life, that I might enjoy all things.

I got nothing that I had asked for, but everything that I had hoped for.
Almost despite myself, my unspoken prayers were answered;
I am among all men, most richly blessed.

ACTIVITIES

1. Invite the catechumens to tell about a time when God answered their prayers or when he didn't answer them as they wished but things worked out well.

2. Read and discuss the prayers of people in Scripture:
   - Abraham bargaining with God to spare a city (Genesis 18:20–32)
   - Moses as he extends his arms in prayer during a battle (Exodus 17:8–13)
   - Hannah longing for a son (1 Samuel 1:9–20)
   - Judith before she ventures into the enemy camp (Judith 9:1–14)
   - Esther before she risks her life to save her people (Esther Addition C 14:1–19)
   - Job when he endures much suffering (Job 40:4–5)
   - Paul writing to the Philippians (Philippians 1:9–11)

3. Give examples of ways that God has spoken to you and invite the catechumens to share their experiences of hearing God.

5

Misconceptions
about Prayer

Some people have incorrect stereotyped ideas about prayer that may make them prayer-shy. In case some of your catechumens do, you might dispel the follow misconceptions

- *Prayer should be long.* **False!** The *Cloud of Unknowing*, a classic book on prayer, says that short prayer pierces the heavens. What do people call out when their house is on fire? They do not scream, "A conflagration is devastating my abode. Please hasten to my assistance." Of course not. They yell one word, "Fire!" Tell the catechumens that their most frequent prayer might be "Help!" St. Augustine said, "A long speech is one thing, a long love another."

- *Prayer should result in a torrent of wonderful thoughts.* **False!** What teen after a date says, "I had a really good time. Look at all the notes I took on what my date said"? That would be ridiculous. Perhaps the grace that comes from prayer is not an idea at all, but a moment of joy, a tear in the eye, a sense of peace, a desire, or a resolution.

- *Prayer should be formal.* **False!** Forget the Thees and Thous. St. Teresa of Avila advises, "Try not to let the prayer you make to such a Lord be mere politeness... avoid being bashful with God." Tevye in *Fiddler on the Roof* is a good example of informal prayer. He shows how prayer should not be regarded as a duty but rather as a visit with a friend. We should pray with the freedom and familiarity of the girl riding a bike who says to God, "If you give me a push, I'll do all the peddling," or the boy who goes to church and shows God, to the consternation of his parents, that he knows how to do a somersault or how to whistle. We don't have to try to impress God with grand words. He knows us through and through and loves us. St. Alphonsus Liguori counsels, "Acquire the habit of speaking to God as if you were alone with him, familiarly and with confidence and love, as to the dearest and most loving of friends."

  By the way, being real and honest with God might mean giving full play to our emotions. This is how the psalmist prayed in the many psalms of lament. For example, repeatedly in Psalm 13 he complained, "How long, O Lord? How long?"

- *Prayer is difficult.* **False!** James Finley recalls, "Merton once told me to quit trying so hard in prayer. He said, 'How does an apple ripen? It just sits in the sun.'" We needn't struggle to pray. Meister Eckhard says, "Get out of the way and let God be God in you." The Jesuit Thomas Greene aptly describes the higher form of prayer as floating as opposed to swimming.

- *I am not worthy to speak to God.* **False!** Every person, though sinful, is a child of God, loved and redeemed by him. Jesus went out of his way to be with sinners. When he was criticized for doing so, he explained that it's the sick, not the healthy, who need the physician.

- *Deep prayer is only for great saints.* **False!** All of us are called to be holy, to be saints. We are all redeemed and baptized. We do not have to be super intelligent or super good in order to experience deep, profound prayer. God showers his gifts, including the gift of prayer, on whomever he wishes.

TIP *Inform your catechumens of this basic principle for praying: Pray as you can, not as you can't.*

Why People Don't Pray

You might ask the catechumens to offer reasons why people don't pray and then discuss them. Among the reasons they suggest might be the following:

I'm too busy and can't find time to pray.

I'm angry at God for something he did or didn't do or allowed to happen.

God never answers my prayers.

God knows what I'm thinking anyway, so why state it?

I'm not sure God exists.

I can't imagine that God cares about someone like me.

I'm afraid God might ask me to do something.

I'd rather pray by doing good deeds.

True Prayer

The test of true prayer is not how good it makes us feel, but how much better we're doing God's will. Prayer makes us more loving, more Christlike. The change in us may be subtle and slow, but it's there. In particular we will show the fruits of the Holy Spirit that St. Paul lists in Galatians 5:22: love, joy, peace, patience, kindness, generosity, faithfulness, gentleness, and self-control.

STORY: *PRAYER BEARS GOOD FRUIT*

A woman was tailgating a car driven by a man. At a yellow light, he stopped instead of speeding through. The woman behind him honked the horn and screamed at him until she heard a tap on the window and saw a police officer. He took her to the police station where she was searched, finger-printed, photographed, and placed in a holding cell. A few hours later, she was escorted to where the arresting officer was waiting with her personal effects. He said, "I'm sorry for this mistake. You see, I pulled up behind your car while you were blowing your horn, flipping off the guy in front of you, and cussing. I saw the 'What Would Jesus Do' and 'My child is an honor student at St. Paul School' bumper stickers and the Christian fish symbol on the trunk. Naturally I assumed you had stolen the car.

TIP *Share with the group your personal prayer stories, how you pray, when your prayers were answered or not, what you have learned about prayer, your favorite prayer, or your favorite way of praying.*

?

Why do Catholics pray to Mary and the saints? Wouldn't it be better to go straight to God?

Because we are all united in the communion of saints and care about one another, Mary and the saints are rooting for us and wish us the best, namely eternal life. Asking them to intercede for us is the same as asking our friends and relatives on earth to pray for us. The saints, however, are more powerful pray-ers than most people on earth because they are the righteous in heaven.

ACTIVITY

Discuss patron saints and give examples such as the following:

Immaculate Conception: the United States
St. Patrick: Ireland
St. Joseph: the universal Church
St. Jude: impossible cases
St. Thérèse of Lisieux: missions
St. Anthony: lost items
St. Cecilia: musicians
St. Thomas Aquinas: Catholic schools
St. Francis de Sales: journalists
St. Lucy: eye afflictions

6

What Jesus Taught
about Prayer

As the Son of God, Jesus enjoyed an intimate relationship with his Father, and so naturally he had a vibrant prayer life. During his life on earth Jesus was a model of prayer for his disciples and for us. In addition, his teachings include specific guidelines for praying.

Jesus modeled prayer for us when he prayed alone and with others. Twice a day Jesus prayed the traditional Jewish prayer the Shema, which begins, "Hear, O Israel, the Lord our God, the Lord is one." He also prayed the psalms both by himself and with others in the synagogue (Luke 4:16) and the Temple. But Jesus also prayed spontaneously, such as when he thanked his Father for his revelations (Matthew 11:25–26). Before undertaking his ministry, Jesus made a forty-day retreat in the desert. The Gospels also show Jesus praying before and during major events in his life:

- during his baptism (Luke 3:21–22),
- before choosing the twelve apostles (Luke 6:12–13),
- before the Transfiguration (Luke 9:28–31),

- before the raising of Lazarus (John 11:41–42),
- and in the garden before his passion and death (Mark 14:32–36).

Jesus prayed early in the morning while it was still dark (Mark 1:35). Sometimes he even prayed all night (Luke 6:12), considered quite a feat by those of us who find one hour a challenge. Jesus prayed before meals (John 6:11, Luke 22:17–19). And he prayed for his friend Peter (Luke 22:31–32). At the Last Supper Jesus prayed for all of his disciples and all of us (John 17:1–26). Finally, Jesus prayed while he was hanging on the cross (Luke 23:34; Mark 15:34, which is a psalm verse; Luke 23:46).

Besides being a model of prayer, Jesus taught several lessons on prayer. He pointed out that we are not to pray in a showy, hypocritical way. Rather, we are to go to our room, close the door, and pray to our Father in secret. He said that we are not to babble but to keep our prayers short and simple (Matthew 6:5–7). Encouragingly, Jesus taught, "Ask, and it will be given you; search, and you will find; knock, and the door will be opened for you" (Matthew 7:7). He assured us that whatever we ask for the Father in his name we will receive (John 16:23), which is why so many of our prayers conclude with a phrase like "through Christ our Lord." Jesus also warned that not everyone who prays, "Lord, Lord," will enter heaven, but the ones who do his Father's will (Matthew 7:21). And, surprisingly, Jesus told us to pray for those who persecute us (Matthew 5:44), an act that changes either them or us.

Parable on Humble Prayer

In one parable Jesus taught us not to boast in prayer, but to be humble. In this parable two men are praying in the

Temple. One is a Pharisee, a protector of the Law. The other is a tax collector, whose profession was associated with theft and Rome, the pagan oppressor. The Pharisee boasts of his good deeds and gives thanks that he is not like sinners such as the tax collector. Meanwhile the tax collector beats his breast and can't even look up as he prays, "God, be merciful to me, a sinner." The tax collector's prayer was more pleasing to God (Luke 18:9–14).

Parables on Persevering Prayer

Two of Jesus' parables have the theme of perseverance in prayer. One of these (Luke 11:5–8) is about a man who has an unexpected visitor in the middle of the night and goes to his neighbor to beg bread so he can be hospitable. He persistently pounds on the door until the neighbor relents and gives him bread. In the other parable (Luke 18:2–8) a widow who is being treated unjustly pleads with a judge to hear her case. Although the judge is a harsh man, he gives in to her just to stop her from hounding him.

STORY: *ST. MONICA*

St. Monica, who lived in North Africa in the fourth century, is a model of persevering in prayer. She was married to an older man who had a violent temper. Her mother-in-law, who also was a difficult person, lived with them. Through Monica's prayers, both her husband and mother-in-law became Christians. Later, Monica's son Augustine led an immoral life and followed a heresy. For seventeen years Monica prayed for his conversion. Eventually Augustine was baptized and became not only a bishop but a saint.

The Our Father

The apostles noticed how absorbed Jesus was when he prayed, and they asked him to teach them to pray. That's when Jesus gave us the gift of the Our Father, or the Lord's Prayer. This prayer wasn't what Jesus prayed because in it we say, "Forgive us our trespasses," and Jesus was sinless. Because the Our Father is from the lips of Jesus himself it is very precious to Christians. After the third scrutiny of the RCIA process, the catechumens will be presented with the Our Father as a gift. Pope John XXIII said, "To know how to say the Our Father and to know how to put it into practice, this is the perfection of the Christian life." It follows that it is worth taking time to explain this prayer.

The basic structure of the Our Father is seven petitions. Three of them refer to God, and four to people. The prayer uses first-person plural pronouns, indicating that it is meant to be prayed together or at least while being conscious of the whole Body of Christ. Here is a simple explanation of the words:

Our Father: We dare to address God as Jesus did, familiarly as our Father. Because the Father, Son, and Holy Spirit are one, we are addressing the whole Trinity. The "our" signifies our communion with all other believers.

who art in heaven: Where God is—there is justice and perfect happiness. Heaven is our homeland and already exists in the hearts of the just.

hallowed be thy name: Hallowed means holy or blessed. A person's name stands for the person himself or herself. In this statement we glorify God and ask that everyone live in a way that hallows God.

Thy kingdom come: God's kingdom or reign is one of peace, justice, and love. We pray that it will spread throughout the world. We pray for the final coming of Christ and the fullness of the kingdom.

Thy will be done: We pray that people will follow God's all-wise plan.

on earth as it is in heaven: In heaven angels and saints constantly do what is pleasing to God.

Give us this day our daily bread: Bread stands for what we need to live. We depend on the good God for all of our necessities. This bread can also signify the Eucharist.

And forgive us our trespasses: We ask God to forgive our sins and failings.

As we forgive those who trespass against us: A dangerous petition because we ask God to forgive us to the extent that we forgive others.

And lead us not into temptation: We ask God to help us discern what is wrong and to keep us safe from people, places, or things that may lead us to sin.

But deliver us from evil: We petition God to protect us from evil, or the Evil One.

?

Why don't Catholics pray the ending phrase to the Our Father as the Protestants do: "For thine is the kingdom, the power, and the glory, forever and ever"?

This doxology, or prayer of praise, is only found in later versions of the Gospel of Matthew. Although Catholics don't regard it as integral to the prayer, during Mass the community prays, "For the kingdom, the power, and the glory are yours, now and forever," after the Our Father but with a short prayer separating them.

TIP For a more thorough explanation of the Our Father, see the **Catechism of the Catholic Church**. Its fourth section on prayer is largely a discussion of this prayer.

ACTIVITIES

1. Assign different Scripture references in this chapter for catechumens to look up and read to the class.

2. On the site where tradition holds that Jesus gave us the Our Father, there is a church with more than sixty large plaques, each with the Our Father in a different language. Have the catechumens learn the Our Father in another language, perhaps Latin:

> *Pater noster, qui es in caelis,*
> *Sanctificetur nomen tuum.*
> *Adveniat regnum tuum.*
> *Fiat voluntas tua, sicut in caelo et in terra.*
> *Panem nostrum quotidianum da nobis hodie,*
> *et dimitte nobis debita nostra*
> *sicut et nos dimittimus debitoribus nostris.*
> *Et ne nos inducas in tantationem,*
> *sed libera nos a malo. Amen.*

7

Setting the Stage
for Prayer

Some places are more conducive to prayer than others. Most people find it easy to pray in a plane 38,000 feet above the earth when there is engine trouble or extreme turbulence. In ordinary circumstances, however, certain factors promote prayer. Inform your group about them and then incorporate them, if feasible, into your prayer experiences during the sessions.

Making Time for Prayer

It's important to carve out time during the day to nurture our relationship with God through prayer. This is a challenge when our lives are very hectic, but notice how we always find time to do the things we really want to do, such as work out or watch a certain television program. St. Thomas More, chancellor of England in the sixteenth century, used to pray every morning from two to six o'clock! If we don't make an appointment with God for a specific prayer time, but relegate him to spare time, he's likely to get no time. Once we make a habit of praying at a certain time, if we are ever forced to skip it, we will miss it.

STORY: *WAITING FOR GOD*

The American author Flannery O'Connor described waiting for inspiration in a way that also applies to waiting for the Lord to speak. She said, "Every morning between 9 and 12, I go to my room and sit before a piece of paper. Many times I just sit for three hours with no ideas coming to me. But I know one thing: If an idea does come between 9 and 12, I am there ready for it."

Silence

Great things happen in silence. For example, flowers and babies grow, snow falls, and the sun rises. We need silence to calm down, to rest, and to think better. Likewise, we need silence to pray. Jesus says in Scripture, "Listen! I am standing at the door, knocking; if you hear my voice and open the door, I will come to you" (Revelation 3:20). Let the catechumens know that God doesn't pound. He knocks. We won't hear him knocking if we always have radios or cell phones over our ears. Or if our mind is not quiet but buzzing with thoughts. We need silence to hear God's soft voice. In Psalm 46:10 we read, "Be still and know that I am God!"

Encourage the catechumens to choose the best time of the day for them to pray, if they haven't already done so, and then to be faithful to this time.

STORY: *GOD SPEAKS IN SILENCE*

Tell or read the story of the prophet Elijah in 1 Kings 19:11–13. God directs Elijah to go stand on the mountain and God will pass by. On the mountain a strong wind comes, but God is not in the wind. Then there's an earthquake, but God isn't in the earthquake. Then there is a fire, but God isn't in the fire. Finally there is only sheer silence, and God speaks to Elijah in that.

Solitude

Jesus often went apart by himself to pray. We sometimes need to be alone with God for a close, intimate conversation, someplace where other people won't distract us.

One woman drives her car to a quiet street and parks to pray. When we are in a crowded room or on a bus we can be "alone" by closing our eyes.

A Special Place

It helps to have a special prayer place where we automatically fall into a mood for prayer. We might have a chair that is our "prayer chair." The place where we meet God could be a certain room in the house, a place outside, a spot in the park, a chapel, the library, or a bench by the lake. This sanctuary can be only in our mind. We can mentally construct a room designed in our favorite colors, furnished with our preferred kind of chairs, decorated with paintings and objects. It might have a picture window with a spectacular view or a blazing fire in the fireplace. In our imagination we can enter that room, make ourselves comfortable, and then envision Jesus joining us.

Ambience

We are creatures with five senses, so it helps to make use of them in creating a good ambience for prayer. Any of the following things will keep us focused on prayer. A Bible is God present in his word. A crucifix reminds us of God's great love for us. A picture or statue of Jesus, Mary, or another saint is also helpful. A burning candle stands for the mystery of God or Christ as the light of the world. Incense (grains or a stick) symbolizes our prayers going to God as its smoke rises. Like incense, potpourri appeals to our sense of smell. A picture of a beautiful nature scene or an item from nature such as flowers, a plant, seashells, rocks, or driftwood can make us think of God's presence. These objects can be placed on a lovely cloth. Some people like to hold a crucifix or other object as they pray. Music is also conducive to prayer.

TIP *Suggest that the catechumens create a prayer corner in their house that includes some of the items mentioned under "Ambience."*

Posture

We can pray while walking, jogging, or bicycling; but prayer is usually associated with kneeling. It's said that St. James had knees like a camel's because he knelt so much. However, St. Dominic is known for his nine ways of praying that are postures and gestures. There's no wrong posture for prayer. We can pray

- standing,
- sitting up straight on a chair (not too comfortably),

- sitting cross-legged on the floor,
- walking,
- running,
- lying in bed,
- prostrate (face down on the floor),
- sitting on a prayer pillow,
- kneeling on a kneeler,
- sitting on our heels, or
- using a prayer stool (a small raised plank on which we sit with our legs under it).

Hands can be folded or resting open, palms up (in an attitude of reception) or palms down on our lap. We can extend our arms in the form of a cross. At times we might raise our arms to God, genuflect, or bow. The Lotus pose is another option: sit with the legs crossed so that the feet rest at the bend of the knees and then rest hands on heels with forefingers and thumbs touching to form a circle. On the other hand, we can dance before the Lord, imitating David who danced before the Ark of the Covenant! Involving our bodies in prayer is praising God with our whole being. Antal Dorati, former conductor of the Washington National Symphony Orchestra, said, "I imagine that the first dance was a movement of adoration…the body simply moving to give thanks to the creator."

TIP *When you are going to hold a prayer experience with your group, as a call to prayer you might use a chime, a rain stick, a gong, or a bell. A rain stick is hollow with pebbles or shells inside so that as the stick is dipped, the items falling inside sound like rain.*

Calming Yourself for Prayer

Teach your group some ways to settle into prayer. Here are some options:

- Do something you find calming. You might walk slowly, listen to music, or crochet.

- Inhale slowly and deeply, count to five, and then exhale slowly. Repeat this three times.

- Relax your muscles. First tighten the muscles on the top of your head for a few seconds and then loosen them. Then do the same in turn for your forehead, eyes, mouth, cheeks, neck, shoulders, arms, hands, chest, thighs, lower legs, and feet.

- Imagine you are floating on a cloud or down a river.

- Become aware of your mind. What is revealed to you?

- Mentally move from one part of your body to another, becoming conscious of the sensations in it.

- Be aware of the air as it passes through your nostrils.

- Listen to the sounds around you. Realize that God is sounding all around you.

- Hold an object. Use all your senses to become fully aware of it.

- Say your name repeatedly as if God is calling you.

Choosing a Name

Addressing God by a particular name at the beginning of prayer helps focus our attention and shape our prayer. Give examples such as Father, Gracious God, Spirit of God, Jesus, Savior, Creator, and then ask for other names, including original names.

Prayer Aids

There are many books available that can be used for prayer. Some are collections of prayers. Others offer a short meditation for each day based on the Scripture readings for the day. You might bring in some samples to show your catechumens. Some Web sites also offer daily devotions, such as www.dailygospel.org and livingwithchrist.us

A Prayer List

It is helpful to list people and intentions that we want to pray for so that we remember them when we pray. The list can be kept in a prayer book or Bible.

ACTIVITIES

1. Have the catechumens estimate how many hours they spend each week grooming, working, eating, talking, sleeping, playing, and traveling. Then have them figure out how much time they spend praying. Their results might induce them to increase their prayer time.

2. Ask the catechumens to describe their favorite places to pray.

8

When *to Pray*

Corrie Ten Boom asks, "Is prayer your steering wheel or your spare tire?" It's normal to pray during times of extreme emotion, such as when we are terrified, sad, or elated. Sometimes prayer comes unexpectedly in a flash—for example, when we behold a breathtaking sunset. Ideally, though, prayer is a daily habit, done as regularly as we take three meals a day. Habits make it easier to do good things, but forming them takes time and persistence. Considering the weighty significance of prayer, it is recommended that we give it our first and best time.

Specific Prayer Times

Most Catholics have a habit of praying at certain times. Here are the three main times for prayer:

In the morning. This is usually our first and perhaps our best time to pray. We are rested, and the concerns of the day haven't yet occupied our minds or used up our hours so there are none left for prayer. In order to pray, some people set their alarm to get up a little earlier. (See the Morning Offering on page 137.)

Before and after meals. We depend on God for our food that keeps us alive. Then it's only courteous to be mindful of him at mealtime. Before meals we ask God to bless our food, and after we've enjoyed our meals we thank him. Meal prayers are called "grace." It's always good to include in meal prayers an intercession for those who do not have enough to eat. (See the prayers before and after meals on page 138.)

In the evening before retiring. At night we thank God for the blessings of the day. We might do an examination of conscience and then pray an act of contrition.

An Examination of Conscience

There are several ways to make an examination of conscience. We might go through the ten commandments and consider whether we have been faithful in keeping each one. Or we might think of each place where we were that day and whether we were loving there: at home, at the office, in the store, at a party, at a game.

Teach your group this Jesuit way of making a nightly examination of conscience. This practice prompts you to make good moral choices during the day because you want to give yourself a positive evaluation at night.

1. Recall God's presence and ask the Holy Spirit to enlighten you.

2. Think of things during that day that you are grateful for, and thank God. These can be small things like a beautiful rose in your garden and the joy of going to a concert or large things like a good report from the doctor.

3. Replay the day like a movie in your mind's eye, looking for times when you accepted God's grace and

times when you didn't cooperate with it. Perhaps you can pat yourself on the back for letting someone take the parking spot you had your eye on or for biting your tongue when tempted to make a hurtful smart remark. On the other hand, maybe you recall with regret how, in the checkout line when the person ahead of you was short of cash, you thought of offering to cover it, but then didn't.

4. Ask forgiveness for your failings.

5. Ask God for grace to respond better the next day. You could look ahead to situations you might face and decide on the best course of action.

STORY: *A RARE PRAYER*

Once a sea captain was caught in a terrible storm. He had weathered many a storm before, but this one was unusually fierce. After desperately trying everything to save the ship, as a last resort the sea captain fell to his knees and prayed, "O God, I haven't bothered you for the last twenty years. Save me and I won't bother you for another twenty."

Sunday: A Day of Prayer

Sunday is our Sabbath, our day of rest. The Hebrew word for rest is *menuha*, which signifies purposeful contemplation, becoming quiet enough to see more deeply into life. Sunday, then is our day for worship—specifically for celebrating Eucharist—and for extra prayer. It's time to listen to God speak in creation, for example, by enjoying our backyard, by visiting a park or a zoo, or by using nature for recreation and going swimming, horseback riding, or skiing. Sunday is also the time to strengthen family and community ties and to do something for those in need. On Sunday we seek creative ways to say to God, "I love you too." As Rabbi Abraham Heschel noted, "The sabbaths are our great cathedrals."

Other Occasions for Prayer

Ask the catechumens for times when our hearts might turn to God. Elicit ideas by naming some of the following instances:

- Facing a crisis
- Making a serious decision
- Dealing with a problem
- On seeing a beautiful sight
- When we are tempted
- After having sinned
- When a friend or relative is sick or in trouble
- On receiving a special blessing
- Before a journey
- On a special day such as an anniversary
- Before an exam or a job interview
- When we're not getting along with someone

Filling Time

Propose using odd moments to pray. Give your catechumens the following examples of down times when they could pray, and then ask for other suggestions.

- On hold on the phone
- Waiting for a red light to change
- Standing in a checkout line
- Waiting for a bus
- Waiting for something to download
- In an elevator
- Waiting for the doctor or dentist
- On the treadmill

Multitasking

Mechanical or repetitive jobs usually require little or no attention, for example, mowing the lawn, scrubbing the floor, and crocheting an afghan. Why not pray at the same time? Some people like to pray on long, monotonous drives or on buses, planes, and trains. According to St. John Chrysostom, "It is possible to offer fervent prayer even while walking in public or strolling alone, or seated in your shop...while buying or selling...or even while cooking."

Pray Always

St. Paul exhorts us to "pray without ceasing" (1 Thessalonians 5:17). We can heed this advice throughout the day by being mindful of God, who is ever mindful of us. An analogy is a husband who is always aware of his beloved although she is working in another room, or even when he is miles away from her. He is with her in remembrance and feeling. Reminders help us think of God—for example, a crucifix on the dashboard of our car or the name "Jesus" printed on a card placed beneath our computer screen. One person has made touching a doorknob a cue for remembering God's presence. God is never farther away than the inner recesses of our own hearts. As the mystic Meister Eckhart once noted, "God is at home. It is we who have gone out for a walk."

St. Teresa of Avila recommended that we experience the Risen Lord by imagining that he is by our side all during the day. We can communicate with him every so often, with or without words. St. Teresa taught, "God walks amid the pots and pans." A seventeenth-century Carmelite lay brother named Brother Lawrence spent most of his life in the kitchen. He disciplined himself to be aware of God to such a degree that he attained great peace and joy and others sought his advice. His instructions are recorded in the classic book on prayer *The Practice of the Presence of God*. Theophane the Recluse summed up this kind of prayer: "The hands at work; the mind and heart with God."

In modern times, the Jesuit scientist Pierre Teilhard de Chardin explained why we could pray always: "God, in all that is most living and incarnate in Him, is not withdrawn from us beyond the tangible sphere; He is waiting for us at every moment in our action, in our work of the moment." Chardin goes on to say that God is "at the tip of my pen my spade, my brush, my needle—of my heart and of my thoughts."

St. Paul himself offers us a way to pray always. In 1 Corinthians 10:31 he advises, "Whether you eat or drink, or whatever you do, do everything for the glory of God." When we offer ourselves and our lives to God, for example by praying the Morning Offering, everything becomes a prayer. By making a conscious effort, our whole life can be prayerful.

TIP *Point out that sometimes while engaged in something, we receive an impulse to pray. We should always try to cooperate with this actual grace as quickly as we answer our cell phones.*

Praying in the Home

The home is rightly called the domestic church. Prayer, therefore, should certainly be part of normal family life. Children learn to pray best by observing their parents pray and by praying with their parents. Some families schedule a time for weekly prayer together and take turns leading the prayers.

→ See #4 on pages 192-194 for ideas for praying at home that you might suggest to your people.

ACTIVITIES

1. To alert the catechumens to their current prayer habits have them write answers to these questions: What three things do you wish for most? What three things are you worried about? What three wonderful things have happened to you lately? Then have the people check which of the nine items they have prayed for specifically. This exercise may be an eye-opener for them, showing them that they may not be taking to God the things that really matter in their lives.

2. Give your people time to think of at least one activity during which they will try to pray. Invite them to share their plans.

9

Difficulties
with Prayer

Some days it is easy to pray, and our prayer leaves us feeling upbeat and renewed. Then there are the other days when we are bored, restless, dry, or plagued by distractions. All we can muster is "Here I am, Lord." Help your catechumens deal with some of the common challenges to faithful prayer. Share with them the comment of Hubert van Zeller: "A lot of the trouble about prayer would disappear if we only realized—really realized, and not just supposed that it was so—that we go to pray not because we love prayer but because we love God." In the end, prayer is a gift. We can take comfort in these words from Scripture: "Likewise the Spirit helps us in our weakness; for we do not know how to pray as we ought, but that very Spirit intercedes with sighs too deep for words" (Romans 8:26). A help to good prayer is realizing that Jesus is not just an idea or a hazy one-dimensional image, but a real, live person. The following are some common challenges to prayer.

Bad Feelings

We don't always feel like praying. But when we're sailing through turbulent times, when we're discouraged, upset, or frustrated is exactly when we need to pray most and when we need God the most. Perhaps we don't feel like praying because we think we "get nothing out of it." But when lovers communicate, they are more intent on giving than on receiving. To persuade your group to ignore negative feelings and persevere in prayer, share this passage from mystic Juliana of Norwich's *Revelation*:

> Our Lord is greatly cheered by our prayer. He looks for it, and he wants it....So he says, "Pray inwardly, even if you do not enjoy it. It does you good, though you feel nothing, see nothing, yes even though you think you are dry, empty, sick or weak. At such a time your prayer is most pleasing to me.

An antidote to dryness in prayer is to pray ready-made prayers. They might spark love in our hearts.

STORY: *STRUGGLES*

One day St. Rita was speaking with Jesus during an apparition and asked, "Lord, on which occasion in my life did I please you most? Was it when I was loving you in ecstasy?" Jesus answered, "No, my dear. You pleased me most on one occasion when you were struggling to complete your daily prayer out of love for me, despite your great desolations."

Distractions

Often when we pray, our minds are very busy or they wander. We flit from one distraction to another. We think about memories, fears, joyful experiences, or what we're going to have for dinner. The Buddhists advise calming "the monkey mind," which darts from idea to idea like a monkey jumping from tree to tree. Sometimes our minds are fastened on one major concern. Maybe we finish praying the rosary and realize that we've spent the entire time thinking about a project we have to do. It is a struggle to focus and refocus on prayer.

There's no need to feel guilty about distractions; they're part of human nature and keep us humble. When a novice was grieving about her distractions, St. Thérèse of Lisieux told her, "I, too, have many, but I accept all for love of the good God, even the most extravagant thoughts that come into my head." Not all distractions are bad. A distraction may be a grace in disguise, for example, if it's the solution to a problem or an idea for an act of charity you can perform. Sometimes distractions during prayer are like thoughts that enter our minds while conversing with friends. In both cases they do not disturb our conversations.

These strategies may help to control distractions:

- Pray at a quiet time in a peaceful place. There will be fewer external distractions.

- Before beginning, recall that you are in God's presence. Make yourself aware of God looking at you with love, and you will be more inclined to focus on him.

- Pray before a crucifix, a picture, or a lighted candle. The visual aid will keep your mind on prayer.

- Write a prayer. This demands concentration and therefore eliminates distractions.

- Pray out loud. This forces you to pay more attention to the words of your prayer.

- If your distraction is important, jot it down so you can deal with it after prayer.

- Ignore the distractions as though they were clouds passing by. Focusing on them only makes them more irritating.

- Work your distraction into your prayer. For example, if you catch yourself thinking and worrying about your mom's upcoming surgery, begin interceding for her.

STORY: *HUMAN NATURE*

A friend boasted to St. Bernard that he never had distractions at prayer. St. Bernard, however, admitted that he had trouble with distractions. One day the two of them were out riding on horseback, and St. Bernard said he would give his friend his horse if he could pray the Our Father without any distractions. The friend began praying aloud. He was doing well. Then after "Give us this day our daily bread" he asked, "Can I have the saddle too?"

Sleeping

Assure your group that it's all right to fall asleep while praying. St. Thérèse of Lisieux explained that she did not regret sleeping during prayer. She pointed out that little children please their parents just as much when they sleep as when they are awake. The heavenly Father loves us as we sleep. We might combat fatigue, however, by eating a candy bar or drinking coffee.

Restlessness

Even St. Teresa of Avila had trouble at prayer. She admitted shaking the hourglass during prayer to speed up the time. Sometimes we're tempted to cut our prayer time short for one reason or another, maybe because we're thinking of all the things we have to do. We need to persevere. One man recounted that when he was inclined to end his prayer early, he forced himself to pray five minutes longer, and during those five minutes he had an extraordinary spiritual experience.

STORY: *THE BUSY COBBLER*

A cobbler asked his rabbi, "What can I do about my morning prayer? My customers are poor people who have only one pair of shoes. I pick up their shoes late in the evening and work on them most of the night so the people have them before they go to work. Sometimes I rush through prayer and get back to work. Other times I skip my hour of prayer. Then I feel bad, and every now and then as I work I can almost hear my heart sigh, 'What an unlucky man I am that I am not able to make my morning prayer.'" The rabbi answered, "If I were God, I would value that sigh more than any prayer."

Busyness

Some days may be so jam-packed that we actually don't pray. A consoling thought, then, is that "the wish to pray is prayer itself" (George Bernanos).

TIP *Explain that anyone who is frustrated or discouraged with his or her prayer life can take heart: One thing we can pray for is the grace to pray well!*

ACTIVITY

Share with the group your own struggles with prayer and invite them to share theirs.

10

Praying with Others

A noted theologian remarked that he could not have gotten through the challenges of recent years without his parish prayer group. Tell the catechumens that some people find great strength in praying together. Suggest that they themselves might want to join, or even start, such a group. Praying together is important, for, after all, our God is a Trinity, three persons. Communal prayer is powerful. Jesus promised, "Where two or three are gathered in my name, I am there among them" (Matthew 18:20). Moreover, witnessing others praying nurtures our own prayer. Another advantage of shared prayer is that bonds form among the group members so that they become a support for one another.

The communal prayer par excellence is the Eucharist, where together as the people of God we praise and thank him. But people also come together for prayers such as the Divine Office, a Holy Hour before the Blessed Sacrament, the rosary, and prayer services, as well as to read, discuss, and pray over Scripture.

Step Prayer

One prayer activity that could be part of a prayer session is the Step Prayer. Have your group form a circle and then turn to face the back of the person to their left. Direct them to take steps one at a time according to your directions. Then read the directions as in the given sample or compose your own.

→ See #5 on page 194 for directions for Step Prayer.

STORY: *FIRESIDE LESSON*

One cold day the village priest went to visit a woman who had stopped going to Mass. As they sat by the fireplace, the woman explained that she realized she didn't need to go to church. She could pray just as well alone in her own home. At that moment the wood in the fireplace shifted and a burning piece of coal rolled out onto the stone floor. The priest and the woman stared at the ember, which, separated from the other hot coals, gradually died.

 TIP Find out what prayer groups meet in your parish and inform your catechumens about them.

Conversational Prayer

Conversational prayer is a form of group prayer begun by Rosalind Rinker and popularized through the Little Rock Scripture Study program. This prayer is carried out as a spontaneous conversation, one or two sentences at a time. It is characterized by directness, simplicity, and brevity. In the beginning the participants introduce themselves and tell a little about themselves. Then they follow these steps of conversational prayer whenever they meet:

1. Recall that Jesus is present and will be guiding your prayer. Picture him and recall his great love for you. Address him: Jesus, I praise you. I love you.

2. Thank the Lord for people, both present and absent, and for their gifts. Thank him for things and events. This step may start by each person giving thanks for those on either side of him or her.

3. Pray for yourself. Ask for specific help and for forgiveness. Respond to others' prayers by praying for them: Lord, help *(Name)* with *(need)*.

4. Pray for others by name. Pray for family, friends, the country, and the world. Give thanks when someone prays for you. Agree with a request: Yes, I pray for that too, Lord.

If you try conversational prayer with your group, encourage them to do the following: Support one another's prayers by responding, "Yes, Lord," "Thank you, Lord," or "Hear this prayer." End with a closing prayer. Relax. Focus on Jesus. Realize that silent moments are all right. Let the Holy Spirit lead you. Address God by any name you wish. Picture God's love coming down on the person you are praying for. Pray with love. Be audible.

Book Discussions

Some people belong to a book discussion group that includes prayer as part of their meetings, perhaps using the book as a springboard. The members all read the same book and then gather once a month to talk about it.

ACTIVITIES

1. Carry out conversational prayer as described in this chapter.

2. Conduct a brief prayer service on a theme, perhaps in honor of a particular feast or a saint. Incorporate a variety of prayer forms: hymns, Scripture, recited prayers, silent prayer.

11

The Eucharist

The Eucharist is our best and most perfect prayer, called the source and summit of Christian life. It is a mosaic of all forms of prayer that together give God the greatest praise and thanks. At Mass, we Catholics gather as the people of God to hear God's Word, to offer Jesus and ourselves to the Father, and to receive Jesus in Communion. Our worship at Mass is accompanied by the worship of all the angels and saints and therefore is a share in the liturgy of heaven. Giving the catechumens an understanding and an appreciation of the Eucharist should be a top priority.

Sacrifice and Meal

The Mass is of infinite value. On the night before he died, Jesus ate a special meal with his disciples. During it he took bread, blessed and broke it, and declared, "This is my body." He passed the sacred bread to his disciples. Then he took a cup of wine, blessed it, and said, "This is my blood of the new eternal covenant." He passed around the cup. Then Jesus commanded, "Do this in remembrance of me." Ever since then the followers of Jesus have been celebrating this memorial meal. We believe that in doing so, the sacrifice of Jesus that saved the world is made present again. This time we are partners in our redemption. At Mass we are able offer Jesus along with ourselves to the Father. Moreover, we believe that the bread and wine, through the power of the Holy Spirit and the actions of the priest, who represents Jesus, truly become the body and blood of Jesus. Therefore when we consume the sacred bread and wine in Communion, we are actually consuming Jesus. We become one with him and one with the other members of the Church who share the same food with us. This meal is a foretaste of heaven where we will enjoy the banquet of eternal life united with God. Blessed Frederic Ozanam, founder of the St. Vincent de Paul Society, claimed, "The best way to economize time is to 'lose' half an hour each day attending Holy Mass."

An Obligation

Explain to the catechumens that the Mass is so crucial to the health of the Church that Catholics are bound to celebrate it every Sunday, which is the Lord's Day. Mention that attending a Saturday vigil Mass is based on the Jewish custom of considering that a day begins the evening before. We also are obliged celebrate Mass on feasts called holy days of obligation, which in the United States are these:

January 1: The Solemnity of Mary, Mother of God

Thursday of the 6th Week of Easter: The Ascension (In most U.S. dioceses the Ascension has been transferred to the following Sunday.)

August 15: The Assumption

November 1: The Solemnity of All Saints

December 8: Immaculate Conception

December 25: Christmas

In years when January 1, August 15, or November 1 falls on a Saturday or a Monday, participation in Mass is optional.

A Communal Prayer

At Mass we come before God as the Body of Christ united in offering prayer and the sacrifice of Jesus. St. John Vianney explained the power of worshiping together: "Private prayer is like straw scattered here and there; if you set it on fire it makes a lot of little flames. But gather these straws into a bundle and light them, and you get a mighty fire, rising like a column into the sky; public prayer is like that."

TIP Mention that out of respect, we fast at least one hour before receiving Communion. That means we take no food or drink except water or medicine. We do not chew gum during Mass. If we haven't received absolution for a mortal sin, we may not receive Communion.

How to Receive Communion

We process up reverently and bow before the priest or Eucharistic minister. We extend our hands with the left one resting on the right one to form what St. Cyril of Jerusalem called a throne for Jesus. In response to the words "the Body of Christ," we respond, "Amen," which means, "I agree." We step aside and using the right hand, place the sacred host in our mouth. An alternate way to receive Communion is to extend the tongue and the sacred host is placed on it. To receive from the cup, we bow and at the words "the Blood of Christ," we respond, "Amen." Then we accept the cup and take a sip of the sacred wine.

Give your catechumens this information:

- It is all right to chew the sacred host as we do regular food.

- After Communion we may speak to Jesus in any way we wish. The word *altar* is an acronym for ideas of what to say: a = adore, l = love, t = thank, a = ask, r = resolve.

- Jesus is present in the sacred host as long as it retains the characteristics of bread.

- We may receive Communion at any Mass we attend.

- Priests as well as extraordinary ministers of Holy Communion may take Communion to the sick and homebound.

?

Why aren't non-Catholics permitted to receive Communion when they attend Mass?

Receiving Communion is a sign that you are one with the Catholic Church and accept all her teachings. A person who is not united with the Catholic Church and who receives Communion would be contradicting the sign value of the sacrament and would not be true to his or her own beliefs. Exceptions are made only with the approval of the bishop. For some Christians the Eucharist is only a symbol of Jesus, whereas Catholics believe Jesus is actually present.

- We should receive Communion at least once a year, preferably during the Easter season.

- Communion services in which we hear Scripture and receive Communion are not equivalent to the Mass, but when it is impossible to celebrate Mass, they are the next best thing.

TIP

Borrow missalettes from your parish so that the catechumens can follow along as you explain each part of the Mass.

Outline of the Mass

Introductory Rites

1. *Entrance procession:* The celebrant and other liturgical ministers process to the altar while the opening song is sung.

2. *Greeting:* All make the Sign of the Cross. Then priest greets us, with a wish that God may be with us.

3. *Penitential rite:* We ask God to forgive our sins that separate us from him and others. Then we will be more spiritually ready to participate in Mass. We pray, "Lord, have mercy."

4. *Glory to God* (except during Advent and Lent): We praise God, beginning by repeating words of the angels on the first Christmas.

5. *Opening prayer:* We pray together silently. Then the priest prays aloud in a prayer prayed in the name of the whole gathered community.

Liturgy of the Word: The Table of the Word

1. *First reading:* This reading, most often from the Old Testament, is in harmony with the Gospel message.

2. *Responsorial psalm:* We respond to God's Word with a psalm.

3. *Second reading:* This New Testament reading is from an epistle or the Book of Revelation.

4. *Alleluia:* We praise Jesus, who will speak to us in the Gospel. This prayer is replaced with another acclamation during Lent, a season when we focus on the passion and death of Jesus and on repentance.

5. *Gospel:* This main reading of Mass is from the Gospel according to Matthew, Mark, Luke, or John. In the Gospel, we hear about the teachings and saving deeds of Jesus.

6. *Homily:* The priest or deacon teaches us about the Scripture readings, relating Jesus' message to our lives.

7. *Creed:* We profess our faith.

8. *General intercessions:* In this prayer of the faithful we pray for the Church, civil authorities, the needy, the salvation of the world, and local needs.

Liturgy of the Eucharist: The Heart

1. *Preparation of the gifts:* Community members bring up the gifts of bread and wine along with water and perhaps donations for the poor and for the Church. The priest prays over the gifts.

2. *Eucharistic prayer:* This prayer is the centerpiece of the Mass. The bread and wine become the body and blood of Jesus (the mystery of transubstantiation) and

his sacrifice on the cross is re-presented.

a. *Preface*—In our name the priest praises and thanks the Father for salvation or some aspect of it.

b. *Holy, Holy*—With the angels we praise God.

c. *Eucharistic prayer*—The priest asks God that the bread and wine may become Christ for the salvation of all who will receive him. He then repeats the words and actions of Jesus at the Last Supper in offering the sacrifice of his body and blood (the consecration). The priest recalls Christ's passion, death, and resurrection. The whole Church of heaven and Earth offers Jesus to the Father with themselves. We pray for all members, living and dead.

3. **Communion Rite:** We receive Jesus under the forms of bread and wine and become one with him and with all church members.

a. *The Lord's Prayer*—We pray for "our daily bread" (the Eucharist), for forgiveness of our sins, and for deliverance from evil.

b. *The Sign of Peace*—We extend peace to those near us, usually by shaking hands and saying, "The peace of Christ be with you."

c. *The breaking of the bread*—While the Lamb of God is prayed, the Eucharist is broken and prepared to be shared with the community. The priest drops a piece of the sacred bread into the cup. Then he shows the sacred host to us, and we pray that God will make us worthy to receive our Lord.

d. *Communion*—The community shares in Jesus' body and blood.

e. *Prayer after Communion*—The priest prays for the effects of the mystery just celebrated.

Concluding Rite

1. **Greeting and blessing:** The priest says, "The Lord be with you," and blesses us.

2. **Dismissal:** We are sent out to love and serve in the world. We thank God. The word *Mass* comes from the Latin sentence *Ite, missa est* (Go, you are dismissed).

 TIP Explain that reading and reflecting on the Scripture readings of the Mass ahead of time is a good way to prepare for Mass.

Church Etiquette

Introduce your catechumens to ritual actions in a church. Explain that for Catholics a church is truly a house of God because we believe that Jesus is with us there in the sacred host reserved in the tabernacle. Near this Blessed Sacrament a candle (sanctuary lamp) burns constantly as a sign that God is present. Out of respect for God, it is customary to genuflect on the right knee and make the Sign of the Cross before entering and when leaving a pew. We also make this act of adoration when passing in front of the tabernacle. When a genuflection is not possible, a reverent bow is made instead. In some parishes genuflecting is no longer practiced.

At the entrances of the church are holy water fonts. On entering and leaving the church, Catholics dip the fingers of their right hand in the holy water and make the Sign of the Cross with it. This is done in remembrance of baptism, when we became Christians and were cleansed of sin.

Gestures and Postures

Explain ways we use our bodies in prayer during Mass:

- Kneeling is an act of humility and adoration before our most high God.

- Standing reflects the dignity we have as human beings and children of God.

- Bowing is an act of humility and reverence.

- During the penitential rite if the "I confess" prayer is used, we strike our breast as a sign of repentance when we say, "I have sinned." Older people may be seen beating their breast at other times, as was the custom before the reform of the Mass.

- When the alleluia or verse before the Gospel is sung, we stand out of respect for Christ in the Gospel.

- When the Gospel is announced we make a Sign of the Cross with our thumb over our forehead, lips, and heart. Mentally we might pray, "Jesus be in my mind, on my lips, and in my heart."

- During the Our Father in many parishes people extend their hands in the "orans," the position the early Christians took when they prayed. It indicates supplication as well as an acceptance of anything God wills. Some people hold hands to express unity. Neither of these is an official practice.

Ministers for the Eucharist

Invite your group to assume a more active role in the liturgy once they are full members of the Church by becoming a special minister: a lector, an extraordinary minister of Holy Communion, an altar server, a greeter, or an usher. They might become involved in music ministry by singing or

THE REAL PRESENCE

There is a story that Fr. Benedict Groeschel, CFR, was riding in a car with a Protestant minister. They passed a Catholic church, and Fr. Benedict made the Sign of the Cross. When the minister asked him why he did this, Fr. Groeschel explained, "Out of reverence for Jesus in the Most Blessed Sacrament." The minister responded, "If I believed what you believe, I would get out of the car, run inside the church, fall on my knees, and never get up again.

playing an instrument, helping to plan liturgies, decorating the church, or assisting the sacristan.

→ See #6 on page 195 for a list of Mass related terms and definitions.

The Church Year

The celebrations of the Eucharist follow an annual cycle based on the mystery of Jesus: the incarnation and his death and resurrection. The church year, or liturgical year, begins with the season of *Advent*, when we focus on the comings of Jesus in history (at Bethlehem), in mystery (in the Eucharist and every day), and in majesty (at the end of time). We joyfully anticipate the Lord's coming. During the *Christmas season* we celebrate the birth of Jesus. This season includes the Solemnity of Mary and the Epiphany. The days after the Christmas season are called *Ordinary Time* because the weeks are numbered with ordinal numbers; for example, there is the Third Sunday in Ordinary Time. In the spring the forty-day season of *Lent* begins with Ash Wednesday. This is a season of penance and preparation for commemorating the passion, death, and resurrection of Jesus. At the end of Lent is Holy Week, with the Holy Triduum days of Holy Thursday, Good Friday, and Holy Saturday/Easter Sunday. The fifty-day long **Easter season**, when we celebrate the resurrection of Jesus, begins with the Saturday night Easter Vigil and concludes with the celebration of Pentecost, when we remember the descent of the Holy Spirit upon the Church. Another period of Ordinary Time follows.

Concomitant with these seasons is the sanctoral cycle of the church year during which we celebrate the feast days of the saints and other special feasts. The prayers of the Eucharist also follow this cycle.

Introduce your catechumens to Catholic prayer traditions associated with the church seasons:

The Advent wreath

The O-antiphons (see page 142)

Receiving ashes on Ash Wednesday

The procession with palm branches on Passion Sunday

Tenebrae

The Good Friday devotions

The blessing of food on Holy Saturday

The Saturday Easter Vigil rites

ACTIVITIES

1. Take your group to the sacristy in your church and show and explain the sacred vessels, books, and vestments used during the Eucharistic celebration.

2. Invite speakers, in particular those who have a special role in the liturgy, to tell what the Mass means to them.

3. Read a list of votive Masses that the priest may offer, which are found in the Sacramentary.

12

Praying with Scripture

The *Constitution on Divine Revelation* (21) states: "In the sacred books the Father who is in heaven comes lovingly to meet his children and talks with them." If prayer is communing with God, what better way is there to enter into it than through God's Word? In the Bible God speaks directly to us in a personal way, revealing himself as a loving God. Reading Scripture, then, is listening to God and thereby coming to know and love him. Swedish Carmelite Wilfrid Stinissen said, "As a rocket fires off a spaceship outside the earth into space, so the word can propel us into God's endlessness." We can use any verses as a launching pad to God by savoring the words and letting them penetrate our hearts. Moreover, the Bible is a gold mine of ready-made prayers that we can adapt to our situations: the Psalms, the Magnificat, and lines like the words of the father asking for his son's healing: "I believe; help my unbelief."

Scripture says about itself, "God's word is living and active, sharper than any two-edged sword" (Hebrews 4:12). It has power to change us. Martin Luther said, "The Bible is alive, it speaks to me; it has feet, it runs after me; it has hands, it lays hold on me." More basically, as someone observed, "A Bible that is falling apart usually belongs to someone who is not." Furthermore, the Bible, especially the four Gospels, helps us to know Jesus. As St. Jerome said, "Ignorance of Scripture is ignorance of Christ." Reading the Bible puts us in touch with Jesus himself, who is called the Word of God. When we introduce catechumens to the treasures of the Bible, we give them the means to enrich their spiritual life abundantly.

For these reasons Pope Benedict XVI called a synod on the Word of God held in Rome in October 2008. Its purpose was that all people may "breathe the richness of Scripture," not only priests and men and women religious but families.

TIP

*Make sure that everyone in your group has a Bible. Help them purchase one if necessary. The **New American Bible** is the version used in Catholic liturgy. The **New Revised Standard Version**, however, is approved for both Catholics and Protestants and has more inclusive language.*

STORY: *FIRST OPENING*

When St. Francis of Assisi was beginning his Franciscan community, he opened the Bible three times and each time found a principle on which to base his rule. Thomas Merton used the same technique when he was deciding whether to join the Trappists (monks who kept strict silence). Merton opened the Bible to the psalm verse "Be silent" (Psalm 46:10). This practice is not superstitious if you approach the Bible as God's Word, prayerfully and with faith and expectancy.

?

What is the difference between Catholic and Protestant Bibles?

Catholics accept more books as divinely inspired than Protestants do, namely Judith, Tobit, Wisdom, Ecclesiasticus, Baruch, Maccabees, and parts of Esther and Daniel. (In addition, Martin Luther questioned Hebrews, Jude, James, and Revelation.) The Hebrew Bible was translated into Greek in 300-200 B.C. in Alexandria, Egypt. This Greek version included some books that were not in the Hebrew Bible. The Protestants and Jews remained with the Hebrew Bible, while Catholics and the Orthodox adopted the Greek version.

Celebrate Scripture

Hold a ceremony to enthrone the Bible. Sing a song about God's Word, process with the Bible and candles, and then place the Bible on a pillow on a special table or shelf. Tell the catechumens that they can also enthrone the Bible in their homes.

→ See #7 on page 197 for a sample enthronement ceremony.

Reading the Bible

Teach various ways to read the Bible:

- *Bit-by-bit:* Read only one or two lines and sink into them, in imitation of Mary, the listening Virgin, who pondered God's ways in her heart.

- *Book-by-book:* Read a book straight through.

- *Bird's eye:* Read only the boldface headings in a book and then reflect on the impact of the whole.

- *One track:* Read according to a theme such as prayer, faith, forgiveness, or justice. Use a concordance or other index to find references.

- *Methodical:* Read the Bible from beginning to end. Larry Anderson said that reading the Bible this way fifty times helped him survive his eight-year captivity in Lebanon.

- *Liturgical:* Read the readings for the day's eucharistic celebration.

- *First Opening:* (sometimes called the lucky dip or Bible roulette) Open the Bible at random and read.

- *Father David Knight's method:* Keep the Bible on your pillow and every night read just one verse. You can always read one verse. Some nights you might read three or four. Before you know it, you'll have read an entire book.

Prayers in Scripture

The Bible contains many prayers that we can repeat. There is Moses' prayer; Daniel's prayer; prayer of Jabez that has become popular (1 Chronicles 4:10); the canticles of Zechariah, Mary, and Simeon; the Lord's Prayer; and prayers in the letters of Paul such as the following:

> I pray that...with the eyes of your heart enlightened, you may know what is the hope to which he has called you, what are the riches of his glorious inheritance among the saints, and what is the immeasurable greatness of his power for us who believe. (Ephesians 1:17–19)

I pray that, according to the riches of his glory, he may grant that you may be strengthened in your inner being with power through his Spirit, and that Christ may dwell in your hearts through faith, as you are being rooted and grounded in love. I pray that you may have the power to comprehend, with all the saints, what is the breadth and length and height and depth, and to know the love of Christ that surpasses knowledge, so that you may be filled with all the fullness of God. (Ephesians 3:16–19)

And this is my prayer, that your love may overflow more and more with knowledge and full insight to help you to determine what is best, so that in the day of Christ you may be pure and blameless, having produced the harvest of righteousness that comes through Jesus Christ for the glory and praise of God. (Philippians 1:9–11)

We have not ceased praying for you and asking that you may be filled with the knowledge of God's will in all spiritual wisdom and understanding, so that you may lead lives worthy of the Lord, fully pleasing to him, as you bear fruit in every good work. (Colossians 1:9–10)

May the Lord direct your hearts to the love of God and to the steadfastness of Christ. (2 Thessalonians 3:5)

I pray that the sharing of your faith may become effective when you perceive all the good that we may do for Christ. (Philemon 1:6)

Of course, then there is also the Book of Psalms, the prayerbook of the Bible.

The Psalms

Dorothy Day, co-founder of the Catholic Worker movement said, "My strength returns to me with my morning cup of coffee and reading the psalms." The one hundred and fifty prayers in this book are prayed by Christians, Jews, and Muslims. Although King David gets the credit for composing the psalms, they actually were composed by various people over the years. The psalms were originally sung, usually in the Temple or on the way to the Temple. Today quite a few favorite hymns are psalm verses in musical settings. Give examples that are familiar to your group, perhaps "For You Are My God" by John Foley (Psalm 16), "Glory and Praise to Our God" by Dan Schutte (Psalms 66 and 67), or "On Eagle's Wings" by Michael Joncas (Psalm 91). There are many song versions of the psalms not only because they are beautiful prayers but because so many of them fit so well in the Mass. Familiarize your catechumens with these prayers, which Jesus and Mary, like all Jews, prayed every day.

 TIP *Give your catechumens a taste of the psalms by presenting some of the most-loved ones: Psalms 8, 23, 91, 121, 139, and 150.*

Point out that footnotes and commentaries help explain the meaning of the psalms. You might give a few examples from your Bible. Teach that the psalms express all the feelings of our heart: praise, thanksgiving, contrition, lament, and love. Because the psalms are poetry, they are chock-full of colorful figurative language, in particular, metaphors and similes. (For example, God is a mountain, he collects tears in a bottle, and enemies are like bees.) However, where our poetry has sound rhyme, the psalms have idea rhyme. A second line in a psalm may echo an idea from the first line in almost identical or different words:

> *The Lord is a stronghold for the oppressed,*
> *a stronghold in times of trouble. (Psalm 9:9)*

> *O Lord, who may abide in your tent?*
> *Who may dwell on your holy hill? (Psalm 15:1)*

It may express the opposite of the idea:

> *For you deliver a humble people,*
> *but the haughty eyes you bring down. (Psalm 18:27)*

Or it can develop the first idea by adding information or relate to the first as cause and effect, question and answer, comparison, or contrast:

> *For the Lord is a great God,*
> *and a great King above all gods. (Psalm 95:3)*

The addition can occur in steps. The second line echoes the first, and a third line carries the idea forward:

> *Lift up your heads, O gates!*
> *and be lifted up, O ancient doors!*
> *that the King of glory may come in. (Psalm 24:9)*

Another type of idea rhyme occurs when a second line contains a simile that creates a picture of the concept in the first line.

> *In the heavens he has set a tent for the sun,*
> *which comes out like a bridegroom from his wedding canopy.*
> *(Psalm 19:4–5)*

TIP *Ask the people to skim the psalms in search of figurative language and share their findings.*

Ways to Pray the Psalms

- Pray the psalm aloud.

- Visualize each image in the psalm.

- After each line pause for a count of four.

- Pray from a Christian perspective: Jerusalem stands for the Church or for heaven, while the king is Jesus.

- Read the footnotes in a Bible in order to better understand a psalm.

- Choose a psalm to fit your situation or emotion.

- Use a psalm to converse, as in this example:

The Lord is my shepherd,
(How grateful I am that you kept me from falling on the ice the other day, Lord.)

I shall not want.
(Thank you for all your gifts, in particular these days a warm house. Please give me a heart that likes to share with others.)

He makes me lie down in green pastures;
(On these cold nights, it's so cozy to be in a warm bed under a comforter and an afghan my mom crocheted.)

he leads me beside still waters.
(Please help those who do not have access to pure water.)

he restores my soul.
(Thank you for the sacrament of Reconciliation the other day. Bless me that I remain filled with your divine life.)

A Way to Pray a Psalm with a Group

After praying the psalm together, individuals add to it in one of three ways: by repeating a line that is meaningful to them, by paraphrasing a verse, or by repeating a verse and adding to it. For example, Psalm 23:1–4 might lead to the following:

Person 1: He refreshes my soul. (repetition)

Person 2: You are at my side. (repetition)

Person 3: He guides me in making the right decisions. (paraphrase)

Person 4: I shall not want anything. I'll have all the peace and love I need. (addition)

Person 5: I fear no evil, not even when people try to ruin my reputation. (addition)

?

How can we pray the cursing psalms when they seem so full of hatred and violence? For example, one says, "Happy shall they be who take your little ones and dash them against the rock!" (Psalm 137:9). Another says, "O God, break the teeth in their mouths" (Psalm 58:6).

The Israelites were very honest with God and freely vented their feelings about their troubles and their enemies. In railing against their enemies, who were pagans, they perceived themselves as fighting for God. However they left their vengeance up to God. Such prayers were an act of faith for them. As Christians we can pray these verses as against our spiritual enemies, our own sins, Satan, evils in the world, or even sickness.

Singing Scripture

Many hymns are based on Scripture passages other than the psalms. Usually a line of print under the hymns in your parish hymnal gives their source. Suggest that the catechumens sing these at home or in the car. Parents might sing them to their children as lullabies.

 TIP *Weave Scripture-based hymns into your sessions and prayer services.*

Reflecting on Scripture

St. Teresa of Avila said, "We have such a great God that a single of his words contains thousands of secrets." Teach the catechumens to pray over just one verse of Scripture. Direct them to consider the literal meaning of each main word, reflect on its meaning for them, and then speak to God about it. They might write their reflections and share them. Here is an example of how to mine Scripture:

"A lamp to my feet is your word" (Psalm 119:105).

Lamp: A lamp enables us to see and carry on our daily activities when it is dark. A flick of the switch floods a room with light. Streetlights guide traffic in the dark; lights guide airplanes and ships. Thank you, God, for the gift of light and the light of your word. May you always be my light. May I walk in the light of your word, and may I be a light for others.

Feet: Usually we don't pay attention to our feet unless they hurt, yet what a service they perform for us. They take us wherever we wish to go. God, guide my feet to good places. Let them hurry to be of assistance to others and to do good.

Word: A word expresses what's in our minds and hearts. It also lets us know what others are thinking and feeling. Because of Jesus, the Word, and Sacred Scripture we are able to know and love God. Lord, let me cherish and understand your word in the Bible and communicate it to others. May I always use it to guide my journey though life.

Receiving a Love Note

Arrange for the catechumens to experience God giving them a personal message. Deliver a Scripture verse on a slip of paper to them by one of the following means.

- Put the papers folded in half in a box, perhaps a heart-shaped candy box. Pass around the box, having each person draw out a verse.

- Curl paper slips using the edge of a scissor blade. Attach one end of each slip inside the outline of a tree, heart, or flower and have the catechumens pluck them.

- Insert the verses into balloons and inflate the balloons. Have the catechumens take a balloon and burst it to retrieve the verse. Or write the verses on inflated balloons, deflate the balloons, and then let each person take one to inflate and read.

- Roll the papers and insert them in bugle snacks.

- Insert the papers into fortune cookies, purchased or homemade. Scripture fortune cookies can sometimes be found in religious goods stores.

- Using thin pastel colored paper, cut out flowers that have five circular petals, each no bigger than the center. In the center of each flower print a Scripture verse with a *permanent* marker. Fold the five petals over the center. Let each person choose a flower and place it on a bowl of water. The petals will slowly open to reveal their verse.

→ See #8 on page 199 for suitable verses to deliver.

Personalizing Scripture

Read aloud Bible passages, or have the catechumens read them, inserting their names or substituting their names for pronouns. Ephesians 1:3–14 with this adaptation is very moving. The hymn to love in 1 Corinthians 13:4–7 makes a good examination of conscience if a person's name is substituted for the word "love."

God might have a personal message for us in the readings on our birthday. Encourage the catechumens to go to Mass on their birthday and pay close attention to the readings that day, or provide a Lectionary and have them look up the readings for their birthday.

→ See #9 on page 200 for Scripture verses to pray in different situations.

Memorizing Verses

Pope John Paul II stated, "The blossoms…of faith and piety do not grow in the desert places of a memoryless catechesis (*Catechesis in Our Time*, 55). Memorized Scripture verses will come to mind when they are needed. Encourage your group to "bank prayers." Share with them these techniques for memorizing verses:

- Reflect on the verse's meaning. Use a dictionary for unfamiliar words.

- Post a verse of the week on a refrigerator or mirror.

- Write the verse several times.

- Sing the verse to a tune.

- Make up motions to accompany the verse.

- If the verse is long, memorize one section at a time.

- Memorize right before you go to bed. The words will stay in your mind better.

ACTIVITIES

1. Ask the catechumens to share times when God has spoken to them through Scripture.

2. Have the catechumens search the psalms for striking similes and metaphors and examples of idea rhyme.

3. Create a moving prayer service by including psalm verses accompanied by beautiful nature scenes flashed on a screen.

4. Hold at least one prayer service that includes Scripture using this outline:
   Song
   Introduction to the theme
   Reading from Scripture
   Psalm response
   Quiet time
   Prayer
   Song

→ See #10 on page 203 for a sample prayer service on repentance.

13

The Divine Office

Your catechumens might know that certain religious orders gather at midnight for prayer and that priests pray from a breviary. Explain that these people are praying the Divine Office, which is also known as the Liturgy of the Hours or Prayer of Christians. The Divine Office is the official daily prayer of the Church. It is part of our liturgy, which is the Church's public worship.

The Liturgy of the Hours parallels the seasons and feasts of the liturgical year celebrated at our daily Masses. A booklet called an *Ordo* is a guide to the feasts and prayers for each day of the year. These are the seven hours of the Office: Morning Prayer, Midmorning Prayer, Midday Prayer, Midafternoon Prayer, Evening Prayer, and Night Prayer. An additional Office of Readings can be prayed at any time. Because the hours of the Office are prayed all over the world around the clock, all time is sanctified.

All Christians are invited to pray the Divine Office, at least Morning Prayer and Evening Prayer (formerly called Vespers), which are called the two hinge hours. In some parishes people pray these prayers together. My own parish prays Morning Prayer each day of the Holy Week triduum.

History of the Divine Office

From Psalm 119:164 we learn that the Jews prayed seven times a day using the psalms. The first Christians, who were Jewish, continued this habit, going to the Temple to pray. After the Christians realized they were a separate religion, they added their own prayers and readings from the New Testament to the hours of prayer. The Divine Office is heavily scriptural.

TIP *Inform your group that at www.universalis.com they can find the entire Prayer of Christians for each day.*

An Outline of the Hours

Morning and Evening Prayer have the following structure. Night Prayer concludes with an antiphon to Mary. Usually for communal prayer the group is divided into two sides, which alternate praying the Scripture verses. The psalms and prayers can be chanted, even on one note.

God, come to my assistance. (Make the Sign of the Cross.)
O Lord, make haste to help me.
Glory to…

Hymn

Antiphon
Psalm, Glory Be, short prayer

Antiphon
Canticle from Scripture, Glory Be, short prayer

Antiphon
Psalm, Glory Be, short prayer

Reading from Scripture
Responsory

Antiphon
Benedictus (Morning Prayer)/Magnificat (Evening Prayer)
Antiphon repeated

Intercessions
Our Father

Prayer of the day
Conclusion: *May the Lord bless us, protect us from all evil, and bring us to everlasting life. Amen.*

You might incorporate parts of the Prayer of Christians in your sessions. For instance, end a session devoted to Mary with the intercessions from the Common of the Blessed Virgin Mary. Giving the catechumens a taste of this prayer

Where can I get a copy of the Divine Office?

A leather cover version called **Christian Prayer: The Liturgy of the Hours** *is available at religious goods stores and Amazon.com.*

might whet their appetites for more. Divine Office books and ordos can be purchased from religious goods stores.

ACTIVITIES

1. Introduce the catechumens to a brief form of one of the hours. For example, you might pray Evening Prayer together to celebrate a certain occasion.

2. Invite someone who prays the Divine Office regularly to explain this prayer or to lead your group in this prayer.

3. Suggest that the catechumens visit a convent or monastery and join the religious there in praying one of the hours.

14

Teaching
Lectio Divina

Lectio divina is Latin for "sacred reading." In 2005, Pope Benedict XVI, speaking about lectio divina stated, "If it is effectively promoted, this practice will bring to the Church—I am convinced of it—a new spiritual spring-time." This prayer method originated with the Fathers of the Church and flourished in Benedictine monasticism. However, it is not just for monks but for anyone. Its four steps, which were defined in the twelfth century, are compared to Jacob's ladder, which connected earth to heaven (See Genesis 28:10–17.) Ultimately this method of prayer leads to union with God. Here are the steps with their Latin names:

1. *Lectio* (reading) Receiving

Choose a passage from Scripture. Read slowly and reverently until an idea attracts you. The words (or word) will jump out at you.

2. *Meditatio* (meditating) Appropriating

Stop and mull over the idea that struck you. Repeat the words over and over, letting them sink into your heart and mind. Delve into the meaning of the words and savor them. Try to discover why those particular words attracted you. When the reason dawns on you, move into the next step.

3. *Oratio* (prayer) Responding

This step takes you from the head to the heart. Respond with a prayer according to how the words prompt you: a prayer of adoration, thanksgiving, sorrow for sin, petition, or love. Stay with these feelings. Let yourself desire God. Put yourself at the disposal of God's Spirit, preparing for God's action. At this point you may return to the passage and continue reading, or you might be lifted by God into the next step, the goal of lectio divina.

4. *Contemplatio* (contemplation) Union

Be with God, enjoying his presence and letting him love you. Be alone with God in the great silence that is too deep for words. Here God takes over your faculties and assumes the lead. It may seem as though nothing is happening, but this is deceptive. Zen wisdom applies to this step: "Sitting still/ doing nothing, spring comes and the grass grows by itself."

(Some people add a fifth step, *operatio*, or action, the change in life that the prayer leads to.)

The first three steps involve doing, while the last one is simply being. The first three are our actions; the last one is God's action. You may repeat steps several times or just do one step. When you are distracted or can't sustain the prayer, return to the passage and read it until another word strikes you. You might share your experiences with another person.

Guigo, a Carthusian monk, summarized the steps of lectio divina this way: "Seek in reading and you will find in meditation; knock in prayer, and it will be opened to you in contemplation." Blessed Dom Columba Marmion, OSB, expressed them like this: "We read under the eye of God until the heart is touched and leaps to flame."

Using lectio divina with Scripture is in keeping with God's command to Joshua to meditate on Scripture day and night (Joshua 1:8). When applied to Scripture, lectio divina has been called "feasting on the Word." The four steps are compared to taking a bite (*lectio*), chewing on it (*meditatio*), savoring its essence (*oratio*), and finally, digesting the Word so that it becomes part of the body (*contemplatio*).

Lectio divina can be used not only with Scripture but also with the following material:

- spiritual books and articles
- prayers
- nature
- the experiences of our lives

An Example

To clarify how to pray lectio divina, you might offer the following example based on Psalm 139.

1. You read the psalm slowly until you come to verse 13b, "You knit me together in my mother's womb." Those words capture your attention.

2. You repeat this verse several times. You begin to meditate on it. You might ponder the ingenuity of God who devised such a mind-boggling way to reproduce

us. You might reflect on the various parts of your body and your talents. You might think about the woman who gave you birth. Suddenly you might come to the realization that God loves you like a mother, even more than your mother loves you. This thought moves you to prayer.

3. You express heartfelt thanks to God for loving you: "O God, your tender love for me is unexplainable. You are so great, and I, more than anyone, know how undeserving I am of your attention and care. Yet, you have shown motherly love for me since the first moment of my existence. Thank you for your goodness and love."

4. As you pray, a strong desire to love God in return may come over you. You may be swept up into an experience where God and you simply enjoy each other's love and presence.

TIP   *Encourage the catechumens to read spiritual books and magazines that will nourish their faith and deepen their relationship with God.*

ACTIVITY

Lead the catechumens through lectio divina in small groups. Light a candle to recall God's presence. Comment that it is all right if they are silent at different steps in the activity. Then guide the prayer through this process:

- In each group one person reads a passage while the rest listen. Then another person reads the passage because people read with different intonations, uncovering different meanings.

- Allow time for a word or phrase to touch everyone's heart.

- Invite the catechumens to reflect aloud. Explain that reflecting differs from discussing. In this case, each person shares thoughts without any response from the others. Some may simply share the word or phrase that has meaning for them.

- Play a related song.

- Invite the catechumens to make a prayer response aloud, one or two simple sentences that their word prompts them to pray. Tell them that it's all right if their response is the same as someone else's.

- Sit in silence for quite some time.

15

Teaching Meditation

Catholic meditation is the direct opposite of the practices of meditation in vogue today as means to relieve stress, get in touch with your inner being, and be healthy. While these modern methods aim to empty the mind, Catholic meditation fills the mind with thoughts of God, Scripture passages, or divine truths. It involves reflecting on these concepts over and over, ruminating on them like an animal chewing its cud. Rick Warren in *The Purpose Driven Life* says that if you know how to worry, you already know how to meditate. When meditating on a Scripture story, consider who, what, why, when, and how. This focused thinking stirs up our emotions and can lead to resolutions for a holier life. Mary is our model for meditation because in Luke's Gospel after the nativity and after the finding of Jesus in the Temple she treasures and ponders the respective events in her heart.

One day I led my ninth graders through a meditation on a Gospel story. The next day as the students filed into class, one asked, "Can we do another meditation?" Others chimed in, saying how much they liked that experience. I was surprised, but then I realized they had probably never meditated before and enjoyed the quiet time focusing on Jesus. Some of your catechumens might be like those students. This chapter offers a few ways you can lead your group into meditation.

Beginning: Quieting and Imagining

First quiet the catechumens. Use one of the suggestions on page 52 under "Calming Yourself for Prayer."

There are different methods for using the imagination to facilitate prayer. In his journal Wordsworth recorded that when he was in a beautiful place, he often imagined Jesus next to him, for instance when he wrote his poem "Daffodils." Once I was in an audience of a thousand people when Father George Maloney, S.J., took us in an imaginary elevator down into the depths of our hearts. He slowly called out the floors as we descended, then left us in silence to commune with God.

Suggest that the catechumens imagine that Jesus is with them. They can speak to him and imagine what he says in reply. Comment that if they are alone, they might speak aloud. Offer these ways that Jesus might be with them:

- Sitting next to them
- Sitting on an empty chair in their room
- Meeting in a room mentally furnished to suit their taste
- Meeting at the seashore, in a lovely garden, or on a mountaintop
- Sitting next to them in a boat
- Walking down a road with them
- Sitting with them in their favorite place

Mention that instead of thinking about God, it is better to think God. In other words, rather than praying by thinking about God and what he's done, focus on God being present to you personally and directly right now.

Ignatian Meditation

St. Ignatius of Loyola developed the *Spiritual Exercises*, a prayer experience that originally was a four-week period under the guidance of a director. Since then the Exercises have been adapted for a week, a weekend, or over several months. In the *Spiritual Exercises*, St. Ignatius taught the following form of meditation, which can be carried out using a Gospel event.

1. Ask for a particular grace.

2. Use your imagination and all five senses to fill in the details of the setting, see the characters and hear them speak, and watch the action. How do you feel toward Jesus in the scene? Replay the event in your mind as if you were participating. For instance, as you meditate on the Nativity, Mary might let you hold the newborn baby for a while. When meditating on the washing of the feet at the Last Supper, you might imagine that Jesus is kneeling to wash your feet.

3. Then discuss the event with God, the Father, the Son, the Holy Spirit, or with Mary. This is called the colloquy.

4. Draw fruit from your reflection by applying the passage to your life and making a resolution.

An Alternate Form of Meditation

Another way to meditate on a Gospel story is to imagine that you are one of the people in the story, experiencing what he or she is experiencing. For example, put yourself in the place of the woman who is caught in adultery, the blind beggar Bartimaeus who is cured, Peter who is invited to walk on the Sea of Galilee, or a child on Jesus' lap.

Here are some Gospel stories that are especially fertile for meditation:

The annunciation of the Lord (Luke 1:26–38)

The boy Jesus in the Temple (Luke 2:41–50)

Temptation in the desert (Matthew 4:1–11)

Calling the first disciples (Luke 5:1–11)

Calming the storm (Luke 8:22–25)

Healing of a leper (Luke 5:12–15)

Healing of a paralyzed man (Luke 5:17–26)

Jesus and the sinful woman (Luke 7:36–50)

Blessing the children (Luke 18:15–17)

Healing a blind beggar (Luke 18:35–43)

Miracle of the loaves (John 6:1–15)

Jesus and Zacchaeus (Luke 19:1–10)

The widow's offering (Luke 21:1–4)

The rich young man (Matthew 19:16–22)

The raising of Lazarus (John 11:1–44)

Driving out the moneychangers (Mark 11:15–18)

The Last Supper (Luke 22:14–23)

Washing the disciples' feet (John 13:1–11)

Agony in the garden (Luke 22:39–46)

The crucifixion (Luke 23:33–49)

On the way to Emmaus (Luke 24:13–35)

A Morsel

Teachers of prayer recommend taking away a morsel from our meditation, a word or phrase to nibble on during the day. This will make our prayer more fruitful and keep us more mindful of God. St. Francis de Sales called this thought to ponder during the day a spiritual nosegay.

Meditating on Art

Looking at a picture, be it a masterpiece or a beautiful nature scene, and reflecting on it is a good way to pray. Icons, those stylized paintings cherished by the Eastern Churches, are called windows into heaven. They give us access to invisible mysteries. While creating an icon, the artist fasts and prays. "The Trinity," "Christ the Pantocrator," and "Our Lady of Perpetual Help" are three well-known icons. Fr. Henri Nouwen's favorite icon was "The Trinity" by Anton Rublev. At a time in his life when he was plagued by despair and fear and unable to pray, he sat for long hours in front of this icon. He wrote, "I noticed how gradually my gaze became a prayer." You might display a picture such as Rembrandt's "The Head of Christ," "Way to Emmaus" by Robert Zund, or even a lovely painting by Monet. Then let the catechumens experience this form of prayer.

Fantasy Prayer

Create a symbolic situation and have the catechumens imagine themselves there. They make choices, act and react, and then analyze their feelings. For example, they can imagine that they meet Jesus in the woods and he gives them a gift. What will he give them? Why? How do they react? Or have them imagine themselves as they were as a baby in a crib. What did the room look like? What did they look like? What were they doing? How do they feel about this baby? Or have them imagine that they are bringing someone to Jesus on a stretcher. Who is it? Why? What do they ask Jesus? How does he reply?

Praying Memories

Invite the catechumens to recall a time when they experienced God's love for them in a special way, when they felt close to God. Have them recall the place, the details of what happened, and how they felt. Then tell them to relive that event in their imagination. Finally, have them speak to God about it.

Healing of Memories

Explain that we can visit painful or bothersome memories and, by reviewing them in the presence of God, put them to rest. Guide the catechumens through these steps:

- Recall that God is present, and rest in him.
- Think about how much God loves you.
- Ask the Holy Spirit to help you recall a past bad experience that negatively impacts your life today.
- Let the memory come to mind.
- Relive the event, this time as though Jesus is there with you. In your imagination let Jesus act and talk to you during the experience.
- Thank Jesus for his love and healing.

ACTIVITY

Lead the group through a guided meditation on a Gospel event as follows:

- Have the catechumens quiet their bodies and their minds.
- Read a Gospel story. Supply helpful background information.
- Tell the story, adding details such as the weather, the setting, and the expressions on people's faces. Make comments that bring the story to life. For example, in telling the story of Zacchaeus, mention that Jesus knew he was in the tree and Jesus also knew the secrets of his heart. In the story of the cure of the blind Bartimaeus, ask what the first thing was that Bartimaeus saw.
- Pose questions based on the story that compel the catechumens to draw meaning for their own lives.
- Allow time for quiet reflection on the questions.

→ See #11 on page 204 for a meditation on Jesus and Zacchaeus.

16

Teaching Mantras

A mantra is a short prayer—a word, phrase, or sentence—
that is prayed repeatedly. Sometimes it is called the prayer
of the heart. The word *mantra* is from the Sanskrit for *man*
(think) and *tra* (liberate). Praying a mantra can free us from
thinking so we can focus on God. Mantras have a long history. Early Christian hermits prayed them to stay anchored
in God. Monks in Egypt continually prayed, "O God, come
to my assistance."

I discovered mantras on my own. One Christmas Day
my sister called with the news that our father had had a
heart attack and had already been anointed. I rushed to
the hospital where Dad was lying unconscious. Tubes were
connected to him, and a respirator was hissing away. This
crisis was especially frightening because no one in our
family had ever been seriously sick before. That night I
couldn't sleep. All of a sudden I found myself saying the
words "The Lord is my shepherd" from Psalm 23 over and
over. The words echoed in my heart and calmed me with a
sense of God's presence. Eventually I slept. The next morning when I returned to the hospital in my father's room I

was introduced to a male nurse who had worked overtime throughout Christmas night caring for him. To my astonishment, the nurse's name was Bob Shepard. And, yes, my dad recovered from this heart attack.

When we are too tired, too weak, or too distressed to pray from a prayer book or to formulate our own prayers, we can pray a mantra. This simple way of praying has power to bring us relief and rest, to make us aware of God's consoling presence, and to open us to God. Its repetition is as soothing as the motion of a rocking chair, a swing, or the waves on the shore. The rhythm imitates our breathing and our heartbeats. Praying mantras is like a child incessantly crying, "Mommy, I don't feel good," or a lover tirelessly repeating, "I love you." Gradually the mantras fall away leaving only the presence of God.

Ways to Pray Mantras

Mantras can be prayed anytime, not just in emergencies. It's especially helpful to pray them while waiting for something or while doing a monotonous task. Mantras can be prayed anywhere: in a checkout line, in an airport, in a doctor's office, or in a car. There are various ways to pray them: silently, aloud, singing them, or synchronizing them with your breathing. Some people like to keep track of mantras with rosary beads.

Although mantras can be prayed while walking, running, swimming, or any other activity, it is recommended that you sit relaxed with hands resting on your lap. Close your eyes and breathe deeply, letting all tension flow out of your body and mind. Focus on the Lord dwelling in you and then whisper the verse slowly over and over, listening with love and desire.

As you pray a mantra, a word might change, altering the meaning of your prayer. For example, as you pray, "I love you, O Lord, my strength" (Psalm 18:1), all of a sudden you might realize that instead of praying "my strength" you are praying "my savior." You might ponder the significance of the change.

Reverse Mantras

Some mantras are reverse mantras, that is, rather than words we say to God, they are words that God is saying to us. For example, "Do not be afraid" (Matthew 28:5) is a comforting mantra before a surgery, a job interview, or any other stressful situation. Further examples are Isaiah 41:13, Isaiah 43:1, Matthew 28:20, John 11:25, John 16:33, and 2 Corinthians 12:9.

Sources of Mantras

The Book of Psalms is a goldmine of mantras. However, they can be gleaned from other Bible books as well. See, for example, Isaiah 25:1, Isaiah 64:8, Habakkuk 3:2, Luke 1:47, 1 Timothy 1:17, and John 6:68. Beautiful and meaningful mantras can also be lifted from the Mass prayers ("Heaven and earth are filled with your glory" or "To know him is to live, to serve him is to reign"), others' prayers ("Lord, make me an instrument of your peace"), favorite prayers ("Teach me, Lord, to be sweet and gentle"), or hymns ("Be thou my vision").

A Favorite Mantra

Some saints had favorite short prayers. St. Francis of Assisi often prayed, "My God and my all." Before St. Catherine of Siena died, for forty days straight she repeated, "I have sinned. Have mercy on me." St. Teresa of Avila revealed that during a sickness she clung to the words "Shall we receive the good at the hand of God, and not receive the bad?" (Job 2:10).

The Name Jesus

The simplest, most beautiful prayer is simply to say the name Jesus. This name contains the presence of the Son of God. It is "the name that is above every name" (Philippians 2:9). The Hebrew name Jesus means "Yahweh saves." By calling on Jesus by name, we bring him to us and within us. Repeating the name Jesus as a mantra is very powerful.

The Jesus Prayer

The Eastern Church gave us the Jesus prayer, which dates back at least to the fifth century. Its origin is the plea of the two blind men in Matthew 20:31. The Jesus prayer is repeated continuously and leads to union with God. A manuscript by an anonymous Russian published in 1884 as *The Way of a Pilgrim* recounts how one man made this prayer his own as a way of praying always. In teaching this mystical prayer, suggest that it can be prayed inhaling on the first half and exhaling on the second half.

> *Lord Jesus Christ, Son of God,*
> *have mercy on me, a sinner.*

Taizé Prayer

The monks of an ecumenical, international community in Taizé, France, have made chanted mantras popular. Their prayer sessions combine sung mantras, Scripture, and silence. The Taizé community website gives this explanation of the short songs: "Using just a few words they express a basic reality of faith, quickly grasped by the mind. As the words are sung over many times, this reality gradually penetrates the whole being. Meditative singing thus becomes a way of listening to God." Recordings of Taizé songs are available.

Centering Prayer

Centering prayer is a method of prayer that opens us to the gift of contemplation. It is founded on the belief that God—Father, Son, and Holy Spirit—dwells within us. St. John of the Cross was convinced of this mystery of the indwelling. He exclaimed, "O soul, most beautiful of Creatures who longs to know where the beloved is, you yourself are the very tabernacle where he dwells." Centering prayer is merely giving loving attention to God dwelling within us and letting God do his work in us. It has its roots in the prayer tradition of the church fathers and desert fathers. A fourteenth-century English monk wrote a book on prayer called *The Cloud of Unknowing*. In it he explains that between us and God there is a cloud of unknowing that can't be penetrated by thoughts or anything except longing love. He recommends creating a cloud of forgetting in regard to worldly things and concentrating on piercing that cloud of unknowing with love. This is the goal of centering prayer. Here are the steps to this means to union with God:

1. Decide on a word or phrase that you will use to keep focused on God. You might choose Jesus, God, Abba, love, mercy, amen, listen, peace, my Lord and my God, or I love you. You will keep the same word throughout the prayer period.

2. Quiet down. Sit upright so your head is well supported by your spine. Be comfortable, but not so comfort-

able that you fall asleep. Keep your eyes gently closed so that energy is not wasted seeing. To relax, breathe slowly three times: exhale, take in fresh air, hold it, exhale.

3. Move toward God within you. Think only of God who is living deep within you and ponder God's love for you. Be present to God. Let his overwhelming love and goodness attract you. Rest in God's presence.

4. Respond with your chosen prayer word or phrase. Repeat this prayer word slowly in your mind.

5. Attend to God and enjoy God's presence. When you know you are aware of things other than God, or your find yourself pestered by other thoughts, use your prayer word to gently bring you back. It functions like a tug on a kite string. Don't stop to think about how you're doing. Focus on giving God your loving attention.

6. When you are finished, pray a formula prayer like the Our Father or speak to God to ease the transition out of centering prayer back to the world around you.

TIP

Caution the catechumens that they will probably not feel the presence of God during centering prayer. However, the prayer will deepen their faith and bear fruit in their lives.

ACTIVITIES

1. Recommend that the catechumens pray a mantra during the week. At the next session ask for their reactions.

2. Give your group a taste of Taizé prayer.

3. Lead your group in an experience of centering prayer. Have them each choose a prayer word. Guide them into the prayer as follows:

Sit straight and still. Close your eyes and think only of God dwelling deep within you. Reflect on God's great love for you. Pray with me: "Jesus, I believe that you are present in the center of my being, loving me. In these next few minutes I want to remember that I am all yours. Let me come into your presence. Draw me to yourself, Jesus." Remain still. Repeat your prayer word in your mind. Stay with Jesus who loves you.

17

Teaching Writing as Prayer

As an English teacher I told my students that you don't really know what you think until you write it. Writing is a wonderful channel for prayer. One benefit is that it demands concentration and therefore eliminates distractions. Following are a few methods for writing prayer that you might share with your "students."

Letter to Jesus

Begin a letter "Dear Jesus," and write Jesus whatever comes to mind. Sign it "Love," and your name. Then begin another letter "Dear" and your name. This one will be signed "Love, Jesus." In this second letter let your pen record ideas freely. Don't force them. You may be surprised at what Jesus says to you. If you do this activity daily, you will have a record of your spiritual life. Rereading the letters from time to time will refresh your prayers. You might annotate them as your life changes.

Paraphrasing a Scripture Prayer

Have the catechumens paraphrase prayers in the Bible, such as the Magnificat or one of the psalms. Psalm 23 works well using an image of God other than a shepherd, for example, God is my coach.

Some psalms are acrostics, that is, each verse begins with a consecutive letter of the Hebrew alphabet. Invite the catechumens to write a prayer using the letters of the alphabet or the letters in their names.

Rewriting a Gospel

Choose a Gospel story and read it. Start writing the account as though you were an eyewitness, using first person pronouns and inserting details of what you observed and thought. At the end, maneuver the plot so that you and Jesus are alone. Write the conversation you have with him based on what just happened but linked to your own life. This exercise can be very revealing.

→ See #12 on page 206 for a sample of a personalized Gospel story.

Journaling

A journal is a personal written record of thoughts, experiences, prayers, and blessings. It can be an aid to prayer or even an act of worship in itself. You don't have to be a good writer to keep a journal. Ask your group if anyone keeps a journal, and if so, what benefits they derive from it. They (or you) might mention the following:

A journal can

- be a way to meet our deeper selves, leading us to know and reflect on our beliefs and ideas, our needs and desires, the meaning of our lives.

- help in resolving conflicts and in working through a bewildering situation or feelings.

- heal wounds.

- be a place to examine the past and the present and thereby own them more fully.

- change our self concept.

- give us a chance to freely express ourselves.

Explain how to keep a journal:

- Set aside time for it. When you don't have time to make an entry, jot down keywords on a special calendar.

- Write about the day's experiences and include your reactions.

- Prime the pump by beginning with a starter question or open-ended statement.

- Let the ideas flow out of your mind and copy them. Don't try to control or edit them.

- Keep your journal private and be honest in what you write.

- Periodically reread your journal to see how God has spoken to you and has acted in your life.

TIP Provide books with blank pages for the catechumens to use as journals, especially as they make their journey through the RCIA.

ACTIVITY

Give your catechumens some of the following ideas for jumpstarting journaling.

I feel like a success/failure when…

I like/dislike…

I wish…

I don't care if…

The best thing about me is…

I would like to change…

I am happy/sad when…

Nothing is as important to me as…

I am proud/ashamed of…

My favorite Gospel story is…

I thank God especially for…

In the future I hope to be…

If you could be somebody else, who would you be?

What mistake have you learned from?

How important in your life is religion?

What do you think is your chief fault?

What do you get most excited about?

What emotions are you feeling right now?

What name would you choose to describe you?

Who would you like to take a trip with right now?

What is your favorite place in the world?

What book had an impact on your life?

What is your favorite movie?

What are you most reluctant to write about now?

What is your greatest ethical problem?

What childhood experience helped make you who you are today?

18

Traditional Catholic Prayers

The *Raccolta* is the official book of Catholic indulgenced prayers and practices that was last published in 1898 in Rome. *Raccolta* is Italian for "collection. Traditional prayers have been handed down from generation to generation as a precious legacy. Knowing these prayers by heart makes it easy for Catholics to pray together. You can help your catechumens learn and memorize the traditional Catholic prayers by beginning and ending your sessions with them and by incorporating them into prayer services. Some prayers would make more sense to the catechumens if you explained them first.

 TIP *You might present your catechumens with their own Catholic prayer books or help them purchase them.*

The Sign of the Cross

As Catholics pray this Trinitarian prayer, they trace over themselves a cross, the sign of our salvation. Jesus turned death into life by his sacrifice on the cross. Demonstrate how to make the prayer by touching your forehead, chest, left and right shoulders. Comment that this symbolizes that we are offering God our whole self. Make sure the catechumens use their right hands and touch their left shoulder first. Explain that the Sign of the Cross is first made over Catholics to bless them at baptism. Mention that after making the Sign of the Cross, Hispanics sometimes place their thumb across their forefinger to form a cross and kiss it. Enumerate times when we make the Sign of the Cross:

- We make it before and after prayers.

- Blessings are given by making the Sign of the Cross over someone, sometimes by making a small one with the thumb on the person's forehead.

- When we receive a blessing, we make the Sign of the Cross over ourselves too.

- When entering and leaving church, we making the Sign of the Cross using the holy water at the door in remembrance of our baptism.

In the name of the Father, and of the Son, and of the Holy Spirit. Amen.

The Our Father

The early Christians prayed the Our Father, also known as the Lord's Prayer, three times a day. We pray it during the Mass and the Prayer of Christians (Divine Office). The Lord's Prayer is also is an excellent meal prayer. See page 44 for more information on this prayer.

Our Father, who art in heaven, hallowed be thy name. Thy kingdom come, thy will be done on earth as it is in heaven. Give us this day our daily bread, and forgive us our trespasses as we forgive those who trespass against us. And lead us not into temptation, but deliver us from evil. Amen.

Hail Mary

The first sentence of this prayer is Angel Gabriel's greeting to Mary at the Annunciation. The second sentence is Elizabeth's greeting to her at the Visitation. The Church added the names of Mary and Jesus. People began adding the rest of the prayer, which was approved by the Church at the Council of Trent in the sixteenth century. The Hail Mary is the main prayer of the rosary. Some people have the habit of praying three Hail Marys every night. This prayer in its Latin form, Ave Maria, has been set to music by great composers.

Hail Mary, full of grace, the Lord is with you. Blessed are you among women and blessed is the fruit of your womb, Jesus. Holy Mary, Mother of God, pray for us sinners now and at the hour of our death. Amen.

Doxology

A doxology is a prayer of praise. The Great Doxology is the Gloria of the Mass. This is the shorter one:

Glory to the Father and to the Son and to the Holy Spirit. As it was in the beginning is now, and will be for ever. Amen.

Doxology *(traditional)*

Glory be to the Father and to the Son and to the Holy Spirit. As it was in the beginning, is now and ever shall be, world without end. Amen.

The Apostles' Creed

A creed is a statement of beliefs. The beliefs in the Apostles' Creed can be traced back to the apostles. In one of the rituals of the RCIA process, the catechumens are presented either with the Apostles' Creed or Nicene Creed.

I believe in God, the Father almighty, creator of heaven and earth. I believe in Jesus Christ, his only Son, our Lord. He was conceived by the power of the Holy Spirit and born of the Virgin Mary. He suffered under Pontius Pilate, was crucified, died and was buried. He descended to the dead. On the third day he rose again. He ascended into heaven, and is seated at the right hand of the Father. He will come again to judge the living and the dead. I believe in the Holy Spirit, the holy catholic Church, the communion of saints, the forgiveness of sins, the resurrection of the body, and the life everlasting. Amen.

Nicene Creed

This creed is usually the one prayed at Mass. It was composed at the Council of Nicea in 325 A.D. and revised at the Council of Constantinople in 381.

We believe in one God,
the Father, the Almighty,
maker of heaven and earth,
of all that is, seen and unseen.

We believe in one Lord, Jesus Christ,
the only Son of God,
eternally begotten of the Father,
God from God, Light from Light,
true God from true God,
begotten, not made,
one in Being with the Father.
Through him all things were made.

For us and for our salvation
he came down from heaven:
by the power of the Holy Spirit
he was born of the Virgin Mary,
and became man.

For our sake he was crucified under Pontius Pilate;
he suffered, died, and was buried.
On the third day he rose again
in fulfillment of the Scriptures;
he ascended into heaven
and is seated at the right hand of the Father.
He will come again in glory to judge the living and the dead,
and his kingdom will have no end.

We believe in the Holy Spirit, the Lord, the giver of life,
who proceeds from the Father and the Son.
With the Father and the Son he is worshiped and glorified.
He has spoken through the Prophets.
We believe in one holy catholic and apostolic Church.
We acknowledge one baptism for the forgiveness of sins.
We look for the resurrection of the dead,
and the life of the world to come. Amen.

Come, Holy Spirit

Invoking the Holy Spirit is recommended before reading the Bible or beginning a period of prayer. The Holy Spirit is our advocate and guide whose role is the sanctification of the Church.

Come, Holy Spirit, fill the hearts of your faithful
and enkindle in them the fire of your love.
Send forth your Spirit and they will be created
and you will renew the face of the earth.

O, God, who by the light of the Holy Spirit,

did instruct the hearts of the faithful,
grant that by the same Holy Spirit we may be truly wise
and ever enjoy his consolations.
Through Christ our Lord. Amen.

Acts of Faith, Hope, and Love

Faith, hope, and love are the three theological virtues that have to do with our relationship with God.

Act of Faith

O my God, I firmly believe that you are one God in three divine Persons, Father, Son, and Holy Spirit; I believe that your divine Son became man and died for our sins, and that he will come to judge the living and the dead. I believe these and all the truths which the Holy Catholic Church teaches, because you revealed them, who can neither deceive nor be deceived.

Act of Hope

O my God, relying on your infinite goodness and promises, I hope to obtain pardon of my sins, the help of your grace, and life everlasting, through the merits of Jesus Christ, my Lord and Redeemer.

Act of Love

O my God, I love you above all things, with my whole heart and soul, because you are all good and worthy of all my love. I love my neighbor as myself for the love of you. I forgive all who have injured me and I ask pardon of all whom I have injured.

Acts of Contrition

An act of contrition is prayed during the celebration of

the sacrament of Penance and often at the end of the day to express sorrow for the failings of that day. It's recommended to pray an act of contrition when in danger of death in order to set things straight with God before going to meet him face to face.

Act of Contrition

My God, I am sorry for my sins with all my heart. In choosing to do wrong and failing to do good, I have sinned against you whom I should love above all things. I firmly intend, with your help, to do penance, to sin no more, and to avoid whatever leads me to sin. Our Savior Jesus Christ suffered and died for us. In his name, my God, have mercy.

Act of Contrition (traditional)

O my God, I am heartily sorry for having offended you, and I detest all my sins because of your just punishments but most of all because they offend you, my God, who are all good and deserving of all my love. I firmly resolve, with the help of your grace, to sin no more and to avoid the near occasions of sin. Amen.

Act of Contrition (short form)

O my God, I am sorry for my sins because I have offended you whom I should love above all things. Help me to do penance, to do better, and to avoid anything that might lead me to sin. Amen.

For the Poor Souls

Catholics believe that our prayers can assist those who have passed from this life by shortening their stay in purgatory, a state of purification that makes one worthy of being in God's presence.

Eternal rest grant unto them, O Lord,
and let perpetual light shine upon them.
May they rest in peace. Amen.

Te Deum

This early Christian prayer is used on special occasions. The hymn "Holy God, We Praise Thy Name" is based on it.

You are God: we praise you;
You are the Lord: we acclaim you;
You are the eternal Father:
All creation worships you.
To you all angels, all the powers of heaven,
Cherubim and Seraphim, sing in endless praise:
Holy, holy, holy, Lord, God of power and might,
heaven and earth are full of your glory.
The glorious company of apostles praise you.
The noble fellowship of prophets praise you.
The white-robed army of martyrs praise you.
Throughout the world the holy Church acclaims you:
Father, of majesty unbounded,
your true and only Son, worthy of all worship,
and the Holy Spirit, advocate and guide.
You, Christ, are the king of glory,
the eternal Son of the Father.
When you became man to set us free
you did not spurn the Virgin's womb.
You overcame the sting of death,
and opened the kingdom of heaven to all believers.
You are seated at God's right hand in glory.
We believe that you will come, and be our judge.
Come then, Lord, and help your people,
bought with the price of your own blood,
and bring us with your saints

to glory everlasting.

Save your people, Lord, and bless your inheritance.
Govern and uphold them now and always.
Day by day we bless you.
We praise your name for ever.
Keep us today, Lord, from all sin.
Have mercy on us, Lord, have mercy.
Lord, show us your love and mercy;
for we put our trust in you.
In you, Lord, is our hope:
and we shall never hope in vain.

Act of Consecration to the Sacred Heart
(St. Margaret Mary Alacoque)

O Sacred Heart of Jesus, to you I consecrate and offer up my person and my life, my actions, trials, and sufferings, that my entire being may henceforth only be employed in loving, honoring and glorifying you. This is my irrevocable will, to belong entirely to you, and to do all for your love, renouncing with my whole heart all that can displease you.

I take you, O Sacred Heart, for the sole object of my love, the protection of my life, the pledge of my salvation, the remedy of my frailty and inconstancy, the reparation for all the defects of my life, and my secure refuge at the hour of my death. O Most Merciful Heart, be my justification before God Thy Father, and screen me from his anger which I have so justly merited. I fear all from my own weakness and malice, but placing my entire confidence in you, O Heart of Love, I hope all from your infinite Goodness. Annihilate in me all that can displease or resist you. Imprint your pure love so deeply in my heart that I may never forget you or be separated from you.

I beseech you, through your infinite Goodness, grant that my name be engraved upon your Heart, for in this I place all my happiness and all my glory, to live and to die as one of your devoted servants. Amen.

The Angelus

The Angelus, which takes its name from the first words, is a reminder of the Annunciation of the Lord. Traditionally this prayer was recited three times daily—at 6 AM, noon, and 6 PM—while the "Angelus bell" was tolled.

V. The Angel of the Lord declared unto Mary.
R. And she conceived of the Holy Spirit. (Hail Mary....)

V. Behold the handmaid of the Lord.
R. Be it done unto me according to thy word. (Hail Mary....)

V. And the Word was made Flesh.
R. And dwelt among us. (Hail Mary....)

V. Pray for us, O Holy Mother of God.
R. That we may be made worthy of the promises of Christ.

Let us pray: *Pour forth, we beseech thee, O Lord, thy grace into our hearts; that, we to whom the incarnation of Christ, thy Son, was made known by the message of an angel, may by his passion and cross, be brought to the glory of his resurrection. Through the same Christ our Lord. Amen.*

Queen of Heaven (Regina Coeli)

The Regina Coeli is a Marian Easter prayer. It replaces the Angelus during the Easter season.

Queen of heaven, rejoice, Alleluia.
For He whom thou didst deserve to bear, Alleluia.
Hath risen as He said, Alleluia.
Pray for us to God, Alleluia.

V. Rejoice and be glad, O Virgin Mary, Alleluia.
R. Because Our Lord is truly risen, Alleluia.

Let us pray: *O God, who by the resurrection of Thy Son, Our Lord Jesus Christ, hast vouchsafed to make glad the whole world, grant, we beseech Thee, that, through the intercession of the Virgin Mary, His Mother, we may attain the joys of eternal life. Through the same Christ Our Lord. Amen.*

Memorare

The name *Memorare* is Latin for "remember." This popular prayer to Mary goes back to at least the fifteenth century.

Remember, O most loving Virgin Mary, that never was it known that anyone who fled to thy protection, implored thy help, or sought thy intercession was left unaided. Inspired with this confidence, I fly unto thee, O Virgins of virgins, my Mother. To thee do I come, before thee I stand, sinful and sorrowful. O Mother of the Word Incarnate, do not despise my petitions, but in thy mercy hear and answer me. Amen.

Hail, Holy Queen (Salve Regina)

This Marian prayer probably originated in the tenth century. It is often prayed at the end of the rosary.

Hail, Holy Queen, Mother of Mercy! Our life, our sweetness, and our hope! To thee do we cry, poor banished children of Eve; to thee do we send up our sighs, mourning and weeping in this valley of tears. Turn then, most gracious advocate, thine eyes of mercy toward us; and after this our exile show unto us the blessed fruit of thy womb, Jesus; O clement, O loving, O sweet Virgin Mary.

Consecration to Mary

Though this prayer we entrust ourselves to Mary, knowing she will help us.

My Queen and my Mother, I give myself entirely to you; and to show my devotion to you, I consecrate to you this day my eyes, my ears, my mouth, my heart, my whole being without reserve. Wherefore, good Mother, as I am your own, keep me, guard me, as your property and possession. Amen.

We Fly to Thy Patronage

This prayer is thought to be the oldest one to Mary.

We fly to thy patronage, O holy Mother of God. Despise not our petitions and our necessities, but deliver us from all dangers, O ever glorious and blessed Virgin.

Magnificat

This is Mary's Canticle found in Luke 1:46–55. The Church prays it every day in Evening Prayer of the Divine Office.

My soul proclaims the greatness of the Lord,
my spirit rejoices in God my Savior;
for he has looked with favor on his lowly servant.
From this day all generations shall call me blessed.
The Almighty has done great things for me,
and holy is his Name.
He has mercy on those who fear him in every generation.
He has shown the strength of His arm,
He has scattered the proud in their conceit.
He has cast down the mighty from their thrones,
and has lifted up the lowly.
He has filled the hungry with good things,
and the rich he has sent away empty.

He has come to the help of his servant Israel
for he has remembered his promise of mercy,
the promise he made to our fathers,
to Abraham and his children forever. Amen.

Litany of Loreto

This Marian prayer lists Mary's many titles. It is named for the shrine of Our Lady of Loreto in Italy, where it was prayed as early as 1558.

V. Lord, have mercy.
R. Lord, have mercy.

V. Christ, have mercy.
R. Christ, have mercy.

V. Lord, have mercy.
R. Lord, have mercy.

V. Jesus, hear us.
R. Jesus, graciously hear us.

V. God, the Father of Heaven,
R. have mercy on us.

V. God, the Son, Redeemer of the world,
R. have mercy on us.

V. God, the Holy Spirit,
R. have mercy on us.

V. Holy Trinity, One God,
R. have mercy on us.

Response: *pray for us.*
Holy Mary,
Holy Mother of God,
Holy Virgin of virgins,
Mother of Christ,

Mother of divine grace,
Mother most pure,
Mother most chaste,
Mother inviolate,
Mother undefiled,
Mother most amiable,
Mother most admirable,
Mother of good counsel,
Mother of our Creator,
Mother of our Savior,
Mother of the Church,
Virgin most prudent,
Virgin most venerable,
Virgin most renowned,
Virgin most powerful,
Virgin most merciful,
Virgin most faithful,
Mirror of justice,
Seat of wisdom,
Cause of our joy,
Spiritual vessel,
Vessel of honor,
Singular vessel of devotion,
Mystical rose,
Tower of David,
Tower of ivory,
House of gold,
Ark of the covenant,
Gate of heaven,
Morning star,
Heath of the sick,
Refuge of sinners,
Comforter of the afflicted,

Help of Christians,
Queen of angels,
Queen of patriarchs,
Queen of prophets,
Queen of apostles,
Queen of martyrs,
Queen of confessors,
Queen of virgins,
Queen of all saints,
Queen conceived without original sin,
Queen assumed into heaven,
Queen of the most holy rosary,
Queen of families,
Queen of peace,

V. *Lamb of God, who take away the sins of the world,*
R. *spare us, O Lord,*

V. *Lamb of God, who take away the sins of the world,*
R. *graciously hear us, O Lord.*

V. *Lamb of God, who take away the sins of the world.*
R. *have mercy on us.*

V. *Pray for us, O holy Mother of God,*
R. *that we may be made worthy of the promises of Christ.*

Let us pray. *Grant, we beg you, O Lord God, that we your servants, may enjoy lasting health of mind and body, and by the glorious intercession of the Blessed Mary, ever Virgin, be delivered from present sorrow and enter into the joy of eternal happiness. Through Christ our Lord. Amen.*

Prayer to the Guardian Angel

Angels are pure spirits who worship God and do his bidding. Catholics believe that God has appointed an angel to care for each person. Jesus referred to these guardian angels. (See Matthew 18:10.)

Angel of God, my guardian dear,
to whom God's love commits me here,
ever this day be at my side,
to light and to guard, to rule and to guide. Amen.

Prayer to St. Michael

When Lucifer led some of the angels against God, St. Michael the Archangel successfully led the other angels in battle against them. He is the patron of the Catholic Church and is invoked especially in time of temptation.

Holy Michael, the Archangel, defend us in battle. Be our safe-guard against the wickedness and snares of the devil. May God rebuke him, we humbly pray; and do you, O Prince of the heavenly host, by the power of God cast into hell Satan and all the evil spirits who wander through the world seeking the ruin of souls. Amen.

Morning Offering

Through the Morning Offering, we make our whole day an act of worship by offering it to God. The Holy Father suggests two intentions to pray for each month. These can be found at ewtn.com/faith/papalPrayer.htm.

O Jesus, through the immaculate heart of Mary, I offer you my prayers, works, joys and sufferings of this day in union with the holy sacrifice of the Mass throughout the world. I offer them for all the intentions of your sacred heart: the salvation of souls, reparation for sin, the reunion of all Christians. I offer them for the intentions of our bishops and of all the apostles of prayer, and in particular for those rec-ommended by our Holy Father this month.

Prayer before Meals

Bless us, O Lord, and these thy gifts, which we are about to receive from thy bounty, through Christ, Our Lord. Amen.

Prayer after Meals

We give you thanks, almighty God, for all benefits. You live and reign now and forever. Amen.

Act of Spiritual Communion

At times when we are prevented from receiving Holy Communion, we can make the following act of spiritual communion to express our love for Jesus.

My Jesus, I believe that you are in the Blessed Sacrament. I love you above all things, and I long for you in my soul. Since I cannot now receive you sacramentally, come at least spiritually into my heart. As though you have already come, I embrace you and unite myself entirely to you; never permit me to be separated from you.

Canticle of Zechariah

Zechariah prayed this canticle when his son, John the Baptist, received his name and was circumcised. The Church prays this prayer each day during Morning Prayer of the Divine Office. It is found in Luke 1:68–79.

Blessed be the Lord, the God of Israel;
he has come to his people and set them free.
He has raised up for us a mighty savior,
born of the house of his servant David.
Through his holy prophets he promised of old
that he would save us from our enemies,
from the hands of all who hate us.

He promised to show mercy to our fathers
and to remember his holy covenant.
This was the oath he swore to our father Abraham:
to set us free from the hands of our enemies,
free to worship him without fear,
holy and righteous in his sight all the days of our life.
You, my child, shall be called the prophet of the Most High,
for you will go before the Lord to prepare his way,
to give his people knowledge of salvation by the forgiveness of
their sins.
In the tender compassion of our Lord
the dawn from on high will break upon us,
to shine on those who dwell in darkness and the shadow of
death,
and to guide our feet into the way of peace.

Prayer of Simeon (Benedictus)

Simeon prayed this prayer when he beheld the child Jesus who was being presented in the Temple. (Luke 2:29–32) The Church prays this prayer each day in Night Prayer of the Divine Office.

Lord, now you let your servant go in peace.
Your word has been fulfilled.
My own eyes have seen the salvation
which you have prepared in the sight of every people,
a light to reveal you to the nations and the glory of your people
Israel. Amen.

Litany of the Holy Spirit

Lord, have mercy on us.
Christ, have mercy on us.
Lord, have mercy on us.

Father all powerful, have mercy on us.
Jesus, Eternal Son of the Father,
Redeemer of the world, save us.
Spirit of the Father and the Son, boundless life of both, sanctify
   us.
Holy Trinity, hear us.
Holy Spirit, who proceeds from the Father and the Son, enter
   our hearts.
Holy Spirit, who art equal to the Father and the Son, enter our
   hearts.

Response: *Have mercy on us.*
Promise of God the Father,
Ray of heavenly light,
Author of all good,
Source of heavenly water,
Consuming fire,
Ardent charity,
Spiritual unction,
Spirit of love and truth,
Spirit of wisdom and understanding,
Spirit of counsel and fortitude,
Spirit of knowledge and piety,
Spirit of fear of the Lord,
Spirit of grace and prayer,
Spirit of peace and meekness,
Spirit of modesty and innocence,
Holy Spirit, the comforter,
Holy Spirit, the sanctifier,
Holy Spirit, who governest the Church,
Gift of God, the most high,
Spirit who fillest the universe,
Spirit of the adoption of the children of God,
Holy Spirit, inspire us with the horror of sin,

Holy Spirit, come and renew the fire of the earth,
Holy Spirit, engrave thy law in our heart.
Holy Spirit, inflame us with the flame of thy love.
Holy Spirit, open to us the treasures of thy graces.
Holy Spirit, enlighten us with thy heavenly inspirations.
Holy Spirit, lead us in the way of salvation.
Holy Spirit, grant us the only necessary knowledge.
Holy Spirit, inspire in us the practice of good,
Holy Spirit, grant us the merits of all virtues.
Holy Spirit, make us persevere in justice.
Holy Spirit, be thou our everlasting reward.
Lamb of God, who takes away the sins of the world, pour
down into our souls the gifts of the Holy Spirit.
Lamb of God, who takes away the sins of the world, grant us
the spirit of wisdom and piety.
Come, Holy Spirit! Fill the hearts of thy faithful and enkindle
in them the fire of thy love.

Let us pray. *Grant, O merciful Father, that thy divine Spirit*
enlighten, inflame, and purify us, that he may penetrate us
with his heavenly dew and make us faithful in good works;
through Our Lord Jesus Christ, thy Son, who with thee in
the unity of the same Spirit, lives and reigns forever and
ever. Amen.

The Divine Praises

The Divine Praises were originally composed in 1797
as a means of making reparation for profanity or blas-
phemy. Today this prayer is prayed at the conclusion of
Benediction.

Blessed be God.
Blessed be His Holy Name.
Blessed be Jesus Christ, true God and true Man.

Blessed be the Name of Jesus.
Blessed be His Most Sacred Heart.
Blessed be Jesus in the Most Holy Sacrament of the Altar.
Blessed be the great Mother of God, Mary most Holy.
Blessed be her Holy and Immaculate Conception.
Blessed be her Glorious Assumption.
Blessed be the Name of Mary, Virgin and Mother.
Blessed be St. Joseph, her most chaste spouse.
Blessed be God in His Angels and in His Saints.

O-Antiphons

The O-antiphons, which each begin with "O," address the Messiah by an Old Testament title and ask him to come. They are prayed on the last days before Christmas as the Alleluia verse of the Mass and in Evening Prayer. They form the verses of the Advent hymn "O Come, O Come Emmanuel."

December 16 *O Shepherd Who rules Israel, you Who led Joseph like a sheep, come to guide and comfort us.*

December 17 *O Wisdom that comes out of the mouth of the Most High, that reaches from one end to another, and orders all things mightily and sweetly, come to teach us the way of prudence!*

December 18 *O Adonai, and Ruler of the house of Israel, Who did appear to Moses in the burning bush, and gave him the law in Sinai, come to redeem us with an outstretched arm!*

December 19 *O Root of Jesse, which stands for an ensign of the people, at Whom the kings shall shut their mouths, Whom the Gentiles shall seek, come to deliver us, do not tarry.*

December 20 *O Key of David, and Scepter of the house of Israel, that opens and no man shuts, and shuts and no man opens, come to liberate the prisoner from the prison, and them that sit in darkness, and in the shadow of death.*

December 21 *O Dayspring, Brightness of the everlasting light, Son of justice, come to give light to them that sit in darkness and in the shadow of death!*

December 22 *O King of the Gentiles, and desire thereof! O Cornerstone, that makes of two one, come to save man, whom you have made out of the dust of the earth!*

December 23 *O Emmanuel, our King and our Lawgiver, Longing of the Gentiles, and their salvation, come to save us, O Lord our God!*

December 24 *O You Who sit upon the cherubim, God of hosts, come, show Your face, and we shall be saved.*

19

More Favorite
Catholic Prayers

Prayers written by holy people sometimes express well what we have in our hearts. You might encourage your people to make some of the following prayers their own.

 TIP *Suggest that the catechumens buy a book with blank pages and create their own prayer book in which they collect their favorite prayers.*

Day by Day (St. Richard of Chichester)

Thank you, Lord Jesus Christ,
For all the benefits and blessings you have given me,
For all the pains and insults you have borne for me.
Merciful Friend, Brother and Redeemer,
May I know you more clearly,
Love you more dearly,
And follow you more nearly,
Day by day.

Prayer for Peace
(attributed to St. Francis of Assisi)

Lord, make me an instrument of your peace.
Where there is hatred, let me sow love;
Where there is injury, pardon;
Where there is doubt, faith;
Where there is despair, hope;
Where there is darkness, light;
Where there is sadness, joy.

Divine Master, grant that I may not so much seek to be consoled, as to console; to be understood, as to understand; to be loved, as to love; for it is in giving that we receive, it is in pardoning that we are pardoned, it is in dying that we are born to eternal life.

Take, Lord, and Receive (St. Ignatius Loyola)

Take, Lord, and receive all my liberty, my memory, my understanding, and my entire will. Whatever I have and possess you have given all to me. To you, Lord, I now return it. All is yours. Dispose of it according to your will. Give me only your love and your grace; I will be rich enough; that is enough for me.

To the Holy Spirit (St. Augustine)

Breathe in me, O Holy Spirit,
that my thoughts may all be holy.
Act in me, O Holy Spirit,
that my work, too, may be holy.
Draw my heart, O Holy Spirit,
that I love but what is holy.
Strengthen me, O Holy Spirit,
to defend all that is holy.

Guard me, then, O Holy Spirit,
that I always may be holy. Amen.

Prayer before the Crucifix

Behold, O kind and most sweet Jesus, before your face I
humbly kneel, and with the most fervent desire of soul, I pray
and beseech you to impress upon my heart lively sentiments
of faith, hope and charity, true contrition for my sins, and a
firm purpose of amendment. With deep affection and grief of
soul, I ponder within myself, mentally contemplating your
five wounds, having before my eyes the words which David
the Prophet spoke concerning you: "They have pierced my
hands and my feet, they have numbered all my bones."

Soul of Christ (Anima Christi)

Soul of Christ, make me holy.
Body of Christ, save me.
Blood of Christ, fill me with love.
Water from Christ's side, wash me.
Passion of Christ, strengthen me.
Good Jesus, hear me.
Within your wounds, hide me.
Never let me be parted from you.
From the evil enemy, protect me.
At the hour of my death, call me.
And tell me to come to you
that with your saints I may praise you
through all eternity. Amen.

Prayer for Generosity (St. Ignatius of Loyola)

Lord, teach me to be generous.
Teach me to serve you as you deserve;

to give and not to count the cost;
to fight and not to heed the wounds;
to toil and not to seek for rest;
to labor and not to ask for reward,
except to know that I am doing your will.

Radiating Christ
(John Henry Cardinal Newman)

Stay with me, and then I shall begin to shine as thou shinest;
so to be a light to others.
The light, O Jesus, will be all from you.
None of it will be mine.
No merit to me,
it will be you who shinest through me upon others.
O let me thus praise you, in the way which you love best,
by shining on all those around me.
Give light to them as well as to me;
light them with me,
through me.
Teach me to show forth your praise, your truth, your will.
Make me preach you without preaching—
not by words, but by example
and the fullness of the love which my heart bears to you.

Prayer of Trust (Thomas Merton)

My Lord God, I have no idea where I am going.
I do not see the road ahead of me.
I cannot know for certain where it will end.
Nor do I really know myself,
and the fact that I think that I am following your will
does not mean that I am actually doing so.

But I believe that the desire to please you does in fact please you.

And I hope I have that desire in all that I am doing.
I hope that I will never do anything apart from that desire.

And I know that if I do this,
you will lead me by the right road though I may know nothing
  about it.

Therefore will I trust you always
though I may seem to be lost and in the shadow of death.
I will not fear, for you are ever with me,
and you will never leave me to face my perils alone.

St. Patrick's Breastplate

I bind unto myself today the strong name of the Trinity,
by invocation of the same, the Three in One, the One in Three.
I bind this day to me forever by power of faith Christ's
  incarnation,
His baptism in the Jordan River, his death on the cross for my
  salvation;
His bursting from the spiced tomb, his riding up the heavenly
  way,
His coming at the day of doom I bind unto myself today.

I bind unto myself today the power of God to hold and lead,
His eye to watch, his might to stay, his ear to harken to my
  need,
The wisdom of my God to teach, his hand to guide, his shield
  to ward,
The Word of God to give me speech, his heavenly host to be my
  guard.

Christ be with me, Christ within me,
Christ behind me, Christ before me,
Christ beside me, Christ to win me;
Christ to comfort and restore me;
Christ beneath me, Christ above me,

Christ in quiet, Christ in danger,
Christ in hearts of all that love me,
Christ in mouth of friend and stranger.

I bind unto myself the name, the strong name of the Trinity,
By invocation of the same, the Three in One, and One in
*   Three,*
Of whom all nature hath creation, eternal Father, Spirit, Word;
Praise to the God of my salvation, salvation is of Christ the
*   Lord!*

Learning Christ

Teach me, my Lord, to be sweet and gentle in all the events of
*   life,*
in disappointments,
in the thoughtlessness of those I trusted,
in the unfaithfulness of those on whom I relied.
Let me put myself aside,
to think of the happiness of others,
to hide my little pains and heartaches,
so that I may be the only one to suffer from them.
Teach me to profit by the suffering that comes across my path.
Let me so use it that it may make me patient, not irritable.
That it may make me broad in my forgiveness,
not narrow, haughty and overbearing.
May no one be less good for having come within my influence.

No one less pure, less true, less kind, less noble for having
been a fellow traveler in our journey toward eternal life.

As I go my rounds from one distraction to another, let me
whisper from time to time, a word of love to you. May my
life be lived in the supernatural, full of power for good, and
strong in its purpose of sanctity. Amen.

Serenity Prayer

God, grant me the courage to change the things I can change,
the serenity to accept those I cannot change,
and the wisdom to know the difference. Amen.

Prayer of St. Francis Xavier

O God, I love Thee for Thyself
   And not that I may heaven gain,
Nor yet that they who love Thee not
   Must suffer hell's eternal pain.
Thou, O my Jesus! Thou didst me
   Upon the Cross embrace.
For me didst bear the nails and spear
   And manifold disgrace;
And griefs and torments numberless
   And sweat of agony;
E'en death itself—and all for one
   Who was Thine enemy.
Then why, O blessed Jesus Christ,
   Should I not love Thee well:
Not for the sake of winning heaven,
   Or of escaping hell;
Not with the hope of gaining aught,
   Not seeking a reward,
But as Thyself hast loved me,
   O ever-loving Lord.
E'en so I love Thee, and will love
   And in Thy praise will sing
Solely because Thou art my God
   And my eternal King.

Mary Stuart's Prayer

Keep me, O God, from all pettiness;
let me be large in thought, in word, in deed.
Let me be done with fault-finding
and leave off all self-seeking.
May I put away all pretense
and meet others face to face
without self-pity and without prejudice.
May I never be hasty in judgment
and always generous.
Let me take time for all things,
and make me grow calm, serene, and gentle.
Teach me to put into action my better impulses,
straightforward and unafraid.
Grant that I may realize
that it is the little things of life that create differences,
that in the big things of life we are one.
And, O Lord God, let me not forget to be kind.

Prayer to the Trinity
(Sister Elizabeth of the Trinity)

O my God, Blessed Trinity whom I adore, help me to become utterly forgetful of self, that I may bury myself in thee, as changeless and as calm as though my soul were already in eternity. May nothing disturb my peace nor draw me out of thee, O my immutable Lord! but may I penetrate more deeply every moment into the depths of thy Mystery.

Give peace to my soul; make it thy heaven, thy cherished dwelling place, thy home of rest. Let me never leave thee there alone, but keep me there all absorbed in thee, in living faith, adoring thee and wholly yielded up to thy creative action.

O my Christ, whom I love, crucified by love, fain would I be the bride of thy heart; fain would I cover thee with glory and love thee...until I die of very love! Yet I realize my weakness, and beg thee to clothe me with thyself; to identify my soul with the movements of thine own. Immerse me in thyself; possess me wholly; substitute thyself for me that my life may be but a radiance of thine own. Enter my soul as adorer, as restorer, as Savior!

O eternal Word, utterance of my God! I long to pass my life in listening to thee, to become docile, that I may learn all from thee. Through all darkness, all privations, all helplessness, I crave to keep thee ever with me and to dwell beneath thy lustrous beams. O my beloved star! So hold me that I cannot wander from thy light.

O "Consuming fire," Spirit of Love! descend within me and reproduce in me, as it were, an incarnation of the Word, that I may be to him another humanity wherein he renews his mystery. And thou, O Father, bend towards thy poor little creature and overshadow her, beholding in her none other than thy beloved Son, in whom thou hast set all thy pleasure.

O my Three, my all, my beatitude, infinite solitude, Immensity wherein I lose myself! I yield myself to thee as thy prey. Merge thyself in me, that I may be immersed in thee until I depart to contemplate in thy light the abyss of thy greatness! Amen.

Prayer of Abandonment
(Charles de Foucauld)

My Father, I abandon myself to you. Do with me as you will.
Whatever you may do with me, I thank you.
I am prepared for anything, I accept everything.
Provided your will is fulfilled in me and in all creatures
I ask for nothing more, my God.

I place my soul in your hands.
I give it to you, my God,
with all the love of my heart
because I love you.
and for me it is a necessity of love,
this gift of myself,
this placing of myself in your hands
without reserve
in boundless confidence
because you are my Father.

Sioux Indian Prayer

O Great Spirit
whose voice I hear in the winds,
And whose breath gives life to all the world,
hear me! I am small and weak,
I need your strength and wisdom.

Let me walk in beauty and make my eyes
ever behold the red and purple sunset!
Make my hands respect the things you have made
and my ears sharp to hear your voice.

Make me wise that I may understand the things you have
taught my people.
Let me learn the lessons you have hidden
in every leaf and rock.

I seek strength, not to be greater than my brother,
but to fight my greatest enemy, myself.
Make me always ready to come to you
with clean hands and straight eyes.

So when my life fades, as the fading sunset,
my spirit may come to you without shame.

Prayer for a Right Heart
(St. Thomas Aquinas)

Give me, O Lord, a steadfast heart,
which no unworthy affection may drag downwards;
give me an unconquered heart,
which no tribulation can wear out;
give me an upright heart,
which no unworthy purpose may tempt aside.

Bestow on me, also, O Lord my God,
understanding to know you,
diligence to seek you,
wisdom to find you,
and a faithfulness that may finally embrace you,
through Jesus Christ our Lord. Amen.

Prayer of a Seeker (St. Ambrose)

O Lord
teach me to seek you,
and reveal yourself to me
when I seek you.
For I cannot seek you unless
you first teach me,
nor find you unless
you first reveal yourself to me.
Let me seek you in longing,
and long for you in seeking.
Let me find you in love,
and love you in finding.

Prayer to St. Joseph

*O blessed Joseph, faithful guardian of my Redeemer, Jesus
Christ, protector of your chaste spouse, the virgin Mother
of God, I choose you this day to be my special patron and
advocate and I firmly resolve to honor you all the days of my
life. Therefore I humbly beseech you to receive me as your
client, to instruct me in every doubt, to comfort me in every
affliction, to obtain for me and for all the knowledge and love
of the Heart of Jesus, and finally to defend and protect me at
the hour of my death. Amen.*

20

The Rosary

After the catastrophe of September 11, 2001, Pope John Paul II urged all individuals, families, and communities to pray the rosary "possibly every day, for peace, so that the world can be preserved from the wicked scourge of terrorism." He was echoing the words of Our Lady in her apparitions, most notably at Fatima, Portugal. Outside of the Mass the rosary is arguably the prayer most associated with Catholics. We hang rosaries in our cars, and we are buried with the beads in our hands. A blessed rosary is a sacramental, something whose use brings special graces through the prayers and merits of the Church. Its prayers are compared to a garland of roses offered to Mary—a token of our love for her. The rosary is sometimes called a chaplet, a word that means "crown." You might carry out instruction and activities related to the rosary especially during the months of May, which is dedicated to Mary, and October, the month of the rosary.

According to a legend, Mary gave a rosary to St. Dominic. Actually, Christians were praying on beads a hundred years before he lived. And the mysteries were formulated about

TIP *Rosary-making kits are available from several sources. Having your catechumens make a rosary is a hands-on means to teach them how to pray it. See www.rosaryarmy.com or www.smp.com.*

two hundred years after his time. The Dominicans, however, were great promoters of the rosary.

The rosary has evolved through the centuries. Long ago many people were illiterate and couldn't pray the daily Church prayer, which included the 150 psalms in the Bible. So instead, they prayed 150 Our Fathers (called *Pater Nosters* in Latin), keeping track of the prayers on strings of beads. In Anglo-Saxon, *bede* was the word for "prayer." In the early eleventh century Lady Godiva bequeathed her prayer-chain made of precious stones to a monastery. In the twelfth century, when the Hail Mary prayer was composed and devotion to Mary flourished, people began praying 150 Hail Marys instead of Our Fathers. As they prayed, people meditated on events in the lives of Jesus and Mary, which were called mysteries, one mystery for each decade, or set of ten beads. There were three sets of mysteries: Joyful, Sorrowful, and Glorious. In 2002, Pope John Paul II gave us a fourth set called the Luminous Mysteries or Mysteries of Light, which closes the gap between the Joyful and Sorrowful Mysteries by covering the public life of Jesus. Blessed Mother Teresa of Calcutta observed, "In praying the rosary with devotion we are reliving the life of Christ."

When we pray the rosary, we unite two forms of prayer: While our minds dwell on the mysteries, we say the formula prayers. The rhythmic praying is so peaceful that some people use the rosary when they have trouble sleeping.

STORY: *THE BATTLE OF LEPANTO*

In 1571, when Turkish ships were about to invade Europe, Pope Pius V, a Dominican, called on people to pray the rosary asking for the Blessed Mother's help. On the first of October the fleets met and fought the Battle of Lepanto. Against odds, the Christians won. The pope declared a new feast in honor of Our Lady of Victory, which later became the feast of the Holy Rosary, celebrated on October 7.

By fingering the beads, we involve creation in our prayer: wood, metal, cord, or glass.

Is it wrong to wear a rosary around your neck?

Because a rosary is essentially meant to be prayed, it is not logical or respectful to use it as jewelry. Canon law states that a sacramental is not to be put to secular use. In some cultures, though, people wear a rosary as a sign of their faith. Some people wear one so that it is handy for praying.

How to Pray the Rosary

Make the Sign of the Cross with the crucifix, and if you wish, kiss the crucifix. On the crucifix pray the Apostles' Creed. Then on the single bead pray an Our Father. On the next three beads pray Hail Marys and pray a Glory Be at the end. Then for each decade, pray an Our Father on the single bead, pray ten Hail Marys, and end with a Glory Be.

An optional concluding prayer is the Hail, Holy Queen. (See page 132.)

Another option is to pray after each Glory Be the prayer that the Angel taught the three children at the apparitions of Fatima:

> *O my Jesus, have mercy on us, forgive us our sins, save us from the fires of hell. Take all souls to heaven, especially those most in need of thy mercy.*

STORY: A PRAYER FOR FOOLS?

On a train a university student sat next to an old man who was praying the rosary. The youth remarked, "I don't believe in such silly things. Take my advice. Throw the rosary out of this window and learn what science has to say." "Science? I don't understand," replied the man. "Maybe you can explain it to me." The student offered, "Give me your address and I'll send you some literature." Fumbling in his pocket, the old man drew out his business card. The boy looked at the card and burned with shame. It read, "Louis Pasteur, Director of the Institute of Scientific Research, Paris."

The Family Rosary

Father Patrick Peyton was a dynamic promoter of the family rosary in the United States. He coined the motto "The family that prays together stays together." In May 2006, Pope Benedict XVI exhorted people to intensify the practice of praying the rosary in order to better understand the key moments of salvation history. He advised newlyweds "to make the praying of the rosary in the family a moment of spiritual growth under the maternal gaze of the Virgin Mary."

TIP Let the catechumens know that the rosary can be prayed without a rosary. They can keep track of the Hail Marys on their fingers. There are also decade bracelets and decade rings available.

The Mysteries

Because we meditate on the mysteries, the rosary is called the Gospel on beads. We can also pray our own mysteries, such as the parable mysteries or the miracle mysteries, or mysteries that speak more to us and our lives. It's the custom to pray the traditional mysteries as follows:

Monday, Saturday: Joyful Mysteries

Thursday: Luminous Mysteries

Tuesday, Friday: Sorrowful Mysteries

Sunday, Wednesday: Glorious Mysteries

To insure that we are *praying* and not merely saying the rosary, we might make an intention for the rosary to motivate us. Or we might spend a minute before praying each decade concentrating on the mystery and asking for the grace to grow in a virtue related to it. Anther option is insert a phrase after the word *Jesus* that connects the Hail Mary to the mystery being prayed.

→ See #13 on page 207 for a list of phrases to insert into the Hail Marys.

Joyful Mysteries

1. *The Annunciation:* The angel Gabriel was sent by God to announce to Mary that God had chosen her to be the Mother of Jesus the Savior, the Mother of God. (Luke 1:26–28)

2. *The Visitation:* Mary traveled to help her older relative Elizabeth who was pregnant with John the Baptist. When Elizabeth heard Mary's greeting, she cried out, "Blessed are you among women, and blessed is the fruit of your womb." Mary responded with the Magnificat prayer. (Luke 1:39–45)

3. *The Birth of Jesus:* Mary gave birth to Jesus, wrapped him in swaddling clothes, and laid him in a manger. Angels appeared to shepherds and sang, "Glory to God in the highest heaven, and on earth peace among those whom he favors." (Luke 2:1–20)

4. *The Presentation in the Temple:* Mary and Joseph presented baby Jesus to God in the Temple as the law required. There, Simeon and Anna recognized that Jesus was the Savior. (Luke 2:22–38)

5. *Finding of the Child Jesus in the Temple:* As a twelve-year-old, Jesus remained in Jerusalem after Passover. On the way home his parents discovered he was missing. Three days later they found him in the Temple

listening to teachers and asking them questions. (Luke 2:41–50)

The Luminous Mysteries

1. ***The Baptism in the Jordan River:*** Jesus had John the Baptist baptize him. John saw the heavens open and the Spirit of God descend on Jesus. A voice came from the heavens saying, "This is my Son, the Beloved, with whom I am well pleased." (Matthew 3:17)

2. ***The Wedding at Cana:*** When wine ran out at a wedding, Mary appealed to Jesus and he worked his first miracle. He turned water into excellent wine. (John 2:1–12)

3. ***The Proclamation of the Kingdom of God:*** Jesus proclaimed the good news of God's love and salvation, saying, "The time is fulfilled, and the kingdom of God has come near; repent, and believe in the good news." (Mark 1:15)

4. ***The Transfiguration:*** Jesus took Peter, James, and John up a mountain. While he prayed, his face changed and his clothing became dazzling white. He spoke with Moses and Elijah. (Luke 9:29)

5. ***The Institution of the Eucharist:*** On the night before he was crucified, Jesus shared a meal with his disciples and gave us the Eucharist. He offered himself for us under forms of bread and wine. In the Eucharist he is with us in a special way. (Mark 14:22–26)

The Sorrowful Mysteries

1. ***The Agony in the Garden:*** After the Last Supper, Jesus went to a garden with Peter, James, and John. He

prayed, "My Father, if it is possible, let this cup pass from me; yet, not what I want but what you want." He found the apostles sleeping. (Matthew 26:36–46)

2. **The Scourging at the Pillar:** Pontius Pilate, to satisfy the crowd, had Jesus scourged by the soldiers and then handed him over to be crucified. (Mark 15:6–16)

3. **The Crowning with Thorns:** Soldiers stripped Jesus and threw a scarlet cloak on him. They made a crown out of thorns and placed it on his head. They put a reed in his hand like a scepter. Kneeling before him, they mocked, "Hail, King of the Jews!" (Matthew 27:27–31)

4. **The Carrying of the Cross:** Jesus, weak from being whipped and beaten, could not carry his cross all the way to Calvary. Simon of Cyrene was forced to help him. (Mark 15:20–22)

5. **The Crucifixion:** At Golgotha (Place of the Skull) Jesus was crucified between two criminals. He prayed, "Father, forgive them; for they do not know what they are doing." (Luke 23:33–46)

The Glorious Mysteries

1. **The Resurrection:** Early Sunday morning an angel appeared to two women at Jesus' tomb and said, "Do not be afraid; I know that you are looking for Jesus who was crucified. He is not here; for he has been raised, as he said." The angel sent the women to tell the disciples. (Matthew 28:1–10)

2. **The Ascension of Our Lord:** Jesus led his disciples to Bethany. He blessed them, then went apart from them and was taken up to heaven. (Luke 24:50–53)

3. *The Descent of the Holy Spirit:* When the disciples were gathered together on Pentecost, the Holy Spirit that Jesus had promised came to the Church with signs of fire and wind. The apostles courageously went out and proclaimed the good news, and people of every language understood them. (Acts 2:1–13)

4. *The Assumption of Our Lady into Heaven:* At the end of her earthly life, Mary was taken up body and soul into heavenly glory, as all faithful followers of Jesus will be someday.

5. *The Coronation of the Blessed Virgin Mary:* Mary, the holy Mother of God, reigns in heaven as Queen of All Saints. There she prays for and cares for the members of Christ.

ACTIVITIES

1. Pray the rosary together, at least one decade.

2. Provide blessed rosaries for the catechumens.

3. Let the catechumens know that there are books and pamphlets that offer brief reflections on each mystery.

4. Have the catechumens create their own five mysteries.

21

The Stations *of the* Cross

The catechumens have probably noticed the stations on the walls of your church or on posts in the parish yard. The Stations of the Cross, or Way of the Cross, is a popular devotion especially during Lent. They can be prayed alone or with a group. In praying the fourteen stations, we trace Jesus' steps from his being condemned to death to his burial. Meditating on the supreme sacrifice Jesus made out of love for us moves our hearts to love and gratitude. The following are the traditional stations. Some people conclude with a "fifteenth station" that refers to the resurrection.

First Station: Jesus Is Condemned to Death

Second Station: Jesus Carries His Cross

Third Station: Our Lord Falls the First Time

Fourth Station: Jesus Meets His Mother

Fifth Station: Simon of Cyrene Helps Jesus Carry His Cross

Sixth Station: Veronica Wipes the Face of Jesus

Seventh Station: Jesus Falls the Second Time

Eighth Station: Jesus Consoles the Women of Jerusalem

Ninth Station: Jesus Falls the Third Time

Tenth Station: Jesus Is Stripped of His Garments

Eleventh Station: Jesus Is Nailed to the Cross

Twelfth Station: Jesus Dies on the Cross

Thirteenth Station: Jesus Is Taken Down from the Cross

Fourteenth Station: Jesus Is Laid in the Tomb

 Mention that scriptural Stations of the Cross composed by Pope John Paul II can be found at www.usccb.org/nab/stations.shtml.

History of the Stations

Originally pilgrims walked the path of Jesus' passion and death in the Holy Land. This practice gained a plenary indulgence, which means that all punishment due for sin was cancelled. But not everyone could travel to Jerusalem. Therefore, the Church offered the same indulgence to someone who made the stations elsewhere. In the beginning, the stations were simply wooden crosses. Later, pictures were added. The Way of the Cross can still be made in the Holy Land. Nine of the stations are on the street, and five are within the Church of the Holy Sepulcher, which is supposedly built over Calvary and the tomb of the Lord.

How to Pray the Stations

Booklets provide prayers to say at the stations. Some of these have a specific theme; for example, stations for the sick, stations for women, and stations with Mary. Books are not necessary, though. We can always pray our own prayers at each station. For public stations, usually one person carries the processional cross, flanked by persons carrying lighted candles. The three people and the leader process from station to station. The name of the station is stated, and we genuflect and pray, *"We adore you, O Christ, and we bless you, because by your holy cross, you have redeemed the world."* Then a reflection is made.

The hymn "At the Cross Her Station Keeping" (*Stabat Mater Dolorosa*) is often sung at the Stations of the Cross. It recalls the anguish of Mary, the mother of the Redeemer who followed Jesus to Calvary and stood at the

?

What are indulgences?

After sins are forgiven, some satisfaction is still due, and known as temporal punishment. This satisfaction is either made on earth or, after death, in purgatory. By indulgences the Church can draw on the treasury of good works of Christ and the saints and apply it as satisfaction for sin. The Church attaches an indulgence to certain prayers and practices, which means that they cancel punishment owed. Indulgences can be partial or plenary, that is, erasing part or all of the punishment due. They can be applied to the souls in purgatory. Martin Luther and others objected to the selling of indulgences, which was an abuse carried out by some clergy.

foot of the cross. Here are the first two and last two verses of the hymn:

At the cross her station keeping
Stood the mournful Mother weeping,
Close to Jesus to the last;

Through her heart his sorrow sharing,
All his bitter anguish bearing,
Now at length the sword had passed.

O thou Mother, fount of love,
Touch my spirit from above,
Make my heart with thine accord!

Make me feel as thou hast felt;
Make my soul to glow and melt
With the love of Christ my Lord.

ACTIVITY

Give your group the experience of praying the stations, even if you only have time for very brief ones.

22

More Catholic Devotions

Devotions are optional prayers and practices that people have developed over the centuries to express their faith. The *Catechism of the Catholic Church* encourages devotions because they help us grow in knowledge of the mystery of Christ and they enrich Christian life. At the same time it teaches that these pious expressions should harmonize with and lead to the liturgy, which "is far superior to any of them."

Eucharistic Devotions

In the thirteenth century priests began to elevate the sacred host during Mass. From this sprang the idea that gazing on the sacred host was meritorious. In 1264 the Feast of Corpus Christi (Body of Christ) was instituted and celebrated by processions in which the Blessed Sacrament was carried. Today Exposition, in which the sacred host is exposed in a holder called a monstrance, is a common and popular devotion. People come to gaze on the sacred host and adore Jesus present in this Blessed Sacrament. You might mention that, formerly, the custom was to genuflect on both knees before the exposed Blessed Sacrament, and this custom might still be seen today.

Some churches or chapels have perpetual adoration in which people take turns praying before the exposed Blessed Sacrament day and night. Making a "holy hour" has its roots in Jesus' question to the apostles during his agony in the garden when they fell asleep instead of praying with him: "Could you not stay awake with me one hour?" (Matthew 26:40). There is also the Forty Hours Devotion in which Jesus in the Blessed Sacrament is adored continually for three days. The number forty symbolizes prayer and penance. For example, the Israelites wandered forty days in the desert, and Jesus fasted in the desert for forty days.

STORY: *FORTY HOURS IN THE USA*

Bishop John Neumann of Philadelphia (1811–1860), the first United States male citizen to be canonized (1977), was responsible for promoting the practice of Forty Hours in the United States. At first his suggestion to begin it met with opposition. Other priests pointed out that the anti-catholic sentiment in the country made it risky to expose the sacred host. Then one night when John was working late, he fell asleep at his desk. As the candle on his desk burned down, it charred some papers, but not seriously. When John awoke, he thanked God that the fire was contained. Then the bishop heard God say, "As the flames are burning here without consuming or injuring the writing, so shall I pour out my grace in the Blessed Sacrament without prejudice to my honor. Fear no profanation, therefore; hesitate no longer to carry out your design for my glory." Consequently, in 1853, John introduced the practice of Forty Hours Devotion.

TIP *Suggest making visits to the Blessed Sacrament to strengthen our love for Christ and to make an oasis for ourselves in the midst of a busy day. Unfortunately many churches must now be kept locked, but the catechumens may be able to find a church or a chapel that is open.*

Benediction

Benediction means "blessing." During the rite of Benediction people are blessed with the Blessed Sacrament. For Benediction, first the priest places the sacred host in a monstrance and incenses it while a hymn of praise is sung, such as "O Salutaris Hostia." After a period of adoration, the priest again incenses the Blessed Sacrament and another hymn is sung, such as "Tantum Ergo." The priest then wraps his shoulders and hands in a humeral veil, lifts the monstrance, and silently makes the Sign of the Cross over the people with the sacred host. The service concludes with the Divine Praises. which are on page 141.

The Sacred Heart

Our heart pumps about 100,000 times a day to circulate our lifeblood. For this reason it has come to symbolize the whole of a person. For example, doing something wholeheartedly means doing it with all our being. The heart

Why do Catholics light vigil lights?

When people light a vigil light, or votive light, they make a donation for it and then pray for an intention. The flame symbolizes their prayer rising to God as long as the candle burns.

is also a symbol of love. How fitting, then, that devotion developed to the Sacred Heart of Jesus. The heart of Jesus stands for the total love of Jesus, divine and human. His heart was literally wounded for love of us when a soldier pierced it with a lance as Jesus hung on the cross.

Devotion to the Sacred Heart originated in the twelfth century but became popular after St. Margaret Mary Alacoque, a Visitation nun in France, had visions of the Sacred Heart from 1673 to 1675. On the Feast of the Body and Blood of Christ, Jesus showed her his wounded heart and said, "Behold this heart burning with love for men." St. Claude de la Colombiere, SJ, supported St. Margaret Mary in promoting this devotion. Other Jesuits as well as St. John Eudes continued to promote it. In 1856, the pope set the Feast of the Sacred Heart on the Friday after the Feast of the Body and Blood of Christ, which usually occurs in June, the month of the Sacred Heart.

Although this devotion focuses on the love and mercy Jesus shows toward us, it also involves reparation for sin. In one of St. Margaret Mary's visions Jesus requested that a Communion of reparation be made on the first Friday of every month for nine consecutive months. He entrusted to her twelve promises to those who honor his Sacred Heart. The twelfth promise was salvation for those who make the first Fridays.

→ See #14 on page 208 for the Twelve Promises.

In art the Sacred Heart appears as a wounded heart surrounded by thorns and surmounted by a cross and flames that signify Jesus' burning love for us. Rays emanating from the heart represent his divinity. The Sacred Heart may be alone or Jesus may be pointing to it in his chest or holding his heart in his hand and gesturing toward it.

Wearing or carrying a Sacred Heart badge or wearing a Sacred Heart scapular shows devotion to the Sacred Heart.

The Enthronement of the Sacred Heart is a practice that helps people think of Jesus' unconditional love and enkindles love in return. The enthronement involves consecrating the family to the Sacred Heart. A statue of the Sacred Heart is placed in the home to remind the family members of their consecration. It is promoted by an organization called the Apostleship of Prayer.

The Immaculate Heart of Mary

Devotion to the Heart of Mary evolved through the centuries. Its focus is Mary as our model in faith, humility, and love of God. In 1830, Mary appeared to St. Catherine Labouré and asked to have a medal cast that is known as the Miraculous Medal. It bore her image on one side and on the other side the sacred hearts of Jesus and Mary.

First Saturdays

In her appearances at Fatima in 1917 Mary asked the children Lucy, Jacinta, and Francesco to promote the practice of going to Mass and receiving Communion as reparation for sin for five Saturdays in a row. This is the practice of the First Saturdays.

May Crownings

To honor Mary as queen of heaven and earth, a statue of her surrounded with spring flowers is crowned during a prayer service. This usually occurs in the month of May, which is Mary's month. Formerly the Queenship of Mary was celebrated on May 31. Now it is on August 22.

Divine Mercy

Devotion to Divine Mercy is centered on God's mercy and love for all, in particular, great sinners. People committed to this devotion trust in God's mercy, are grateful for it, and show mercy themselves. This rather new devotion began with St. Faustina Kowalska (1905–1938), an uneducated nun in Poland. She was favored with revelations, which her spiritual director had her record in a diary.

In February 1931, Faustina saw Jesus with one hand raised in blessing and the other touching his white garment at his heart. From that spot came forth two large rays, one red and one pale. Jesus directed Faustina to have an image made of him like this along with the words "Jesus, I trust in you." Later Jesus told her that the rays stood for the blood and water that streamed from his heart when it was pierced.

?

What is a scapular?

A scapular is two small pieces of cloth connected by strings that are worn around the neck in front and in back in imitation of the long scapular of a religious habit. They are a sign of association with the spirituality of a religious order. The most common scapular is the brown scapular of Our Lady of Mount Carmel. Wearing it shows devotion to Mary and the intent to live a Christian life. A person usually receives a scapular from a priest and can only receive it once. Today a scapular medal can be worn instead of a cloth one. The medal shows the Sacred Heart on one side and Our Lady on the other side. Scapulars are sacramentals that have indulgences connected to them.

Jesus also requested that every day at 3 PM, the hour of his death, we remember his great mercy.

In addition, Jesus asked Faustina that the Sunday after Easter be a feast dedicated to the Divine Mercy, and he promised graces to those who receive Communion on this day. He also asked that beginning on Good Friday a novena for this feast be made and gave an intention for each day of the novena. On the day of Faustina's canonization in the year 2000, Pope John Paul II declared that the Second Sunday of Easter would be called Divine Mercy Sunday.

Chaplet of Divine Mercy

A chaplet is a string of prayer beads. Jesus asked St. Faustina to promote the praying of the Chaplet of Divine Mercy, which is prayed on a rosary as follows:

Pray the Our Father, the Hail Mary, and the Apostles' Creed.

Then on the single bead before each decade pray
Eternal Father
I offer you the body and blood, soul and divinity
of your dearly beloved Son, Our Lord Jesus Christ,
in atonement for our sins and those of the whole world.

On the ten beads of each decade pray
For the sake of his sorrowful Passion,
have mercy on us and on the whole world.

Conclude by repeating three times
Holy God, Holy Mighty One, Holy Immortal One,
have mercy on us and on the whole world.

The Infant of Prague

The Infant of Prague devotion focuses on Jesus' childhood and kingship. The statue depicts Jesus as a small child. He is crowned and holds a globe surmounted with a cross. His right hand is raised in blessing. The original statue, eighteen inches high, was brought from Spain and presented to Discalced Carmelite Fathers in Prague, Czechoslovakia, in 1628. During a war, the Fathers left and the statue was broken and tossed with rubbish. When the Fathers returned, Fr. Cyril discovered it behind the altar. One day while praying by the statue Fr. Cyril heard Jesus say, "Have mercy on me and I will have mercy on you. Return my hands to me and I shall give you peace. The more you honor me, the more I shall bless you." Today the statue stands in a gold and glass case at the Church of Our Lady of Victory in Prague. Carmelite sisters change its more than seventy outfits. Copies of the statue can be found in churches and homes today.

→ See #15 on page 209 for a novena to the Infant of Prague.

The Holy Child of Atocha

Devotion to the Santo Niño de Atocha is popular in Spain, Mexico, and the southwestern United States. This Holy Child helps prisoners, travelers, miners, the sick, and now immigrants. Many legends surround the statue of the Santo Niño, beginning somewhere between the 13th and 15th century. When the town of Atocha in Spain fell to the Muslims, Christians were imprisoned and denied food except that brought by children. After the women prayed to Our Lady of Atocha, a child in pilgrim's clothing began bringing food to prisoners. People noticed that on the statue of Our Lady of Atocha, which showed her holding the Child Jesus, his shoes were worn and dusty. Whenever these shoes were replaced, they became soiled again.

Travelers outside of Atocha told how a boy, dressed as a pilgrim, brought them food and supplies. He often traveled with them and guided them to safe roads. Still another story recounts that an explosion in Fresnillo, Mexico, trapped many miners. When their wives went to church to pray, they saw that the child on the statue of Our Lady of Atocha was missing. The miners eventually emerged from the mine and explained that a child had given them water and had showed them the way out. Later, there were other reports of a child helping miners in need. Each time the image of the child on Mary's lap was found to be dirty and his clothes torn.

The Santo Niño de Atocha is usually seated. He wears a wide-brimmed hat and a long ornate cloak. In one hand he holds a basket of roses or food and in the other a pilgrim's staff, which often has a water gourd hanging from it. Later, the Shell of Saint James was added to his cloak because it is a symbol of pilgrimage to the Shrine of St. James in Compostela, Spain.

Month Dedications

Traditionally Catholics have dedicated each month to a certain aspect of the faith as follows:

January: Holy Childhood

February: Holy Family

March: St. Joseph

April: Holy Spirit/Holy Eucharist

May: Mary

June: Sacred Heart

July: Precious Blood

August: Blessed Sacrament

September: Seven Sorrows of Mary

October: Holy rosary

November: Souls in purgatory

December: Immaculate Conception

ACTIVITIES

1. Arrange to have your catechumens participate in Benediction and Adoration of the Blessed Sacrament.

2. Present your catechumens with badges or pictures of the Sacred Heart and pray together the Act of Consecration to the Sacred Heart on page 130.

23

A Potpourri of
Prayer Styles

Down through the ages methods of praying and ways to spark prayer have developed. You might introduce your catechumens to some of the following in order to expand their prayer repertoire.

Praying with Art
Some people use drawing, painting, or sculpting as a means of prayer. The creative action stirs and helps them express their thoughts and emotions. Even doodling can be a springboard to prayer. Doodle on paper and then look for a shape and pray about it.

Pilgrimages
Traveling to a sacred place is known as a pilgrimage. Pilgrimages were especially popular in the Middle Ages. The framework of Chaucer's *Canterbury Tales* is a pilgrimage to the shrine of St. Thomas Becket. Today people make pilgrimages to the Holy Land, where Jesus lived, to Rome,

which is the heart of the Church today, or to a shrine such as Our Lady of Lourdes in France and Our Lady of Fatima in Portugal.

 Encourage your catechumens to make a pilgrimage to a shrine near you. Name some shrines in your area and tell about them if you can. You might arrange for a group pilgrimage.

The Labyrinth

Not everyone could make a pilgrimage to Jerusalem, so in the Middle Ages labyrinths became a substitute. A labyrinth is not a maze because there is only one path that weaves around within a circle and ends at the center. Several European cathedrals had labyrinths in their floors. The only one remaining is the forty-two-foot-wide labyrinth in the cathedral of Chartres. People pray as they walk along a winding path to the center, which represents God. Then they retrace their steps going back out to the world. The path represents the journey of life as it sometimes leads away from God and sometimes has us pass other people. The prayer along the way can vary. We can walk with a Scripture verse, a mantra, a feeling, a question, a petition, or simply walk, paying attention to our thoughts and feelings. The labyrinth can be walked slowly or even danced. We can play during this prayer activity or sing.

Today some labyrinths are constructed outside. If there is an institution nearby that has one, you might visit it with the catechumens. Some institutions have a canvas labyrinth available which you might be able to borrow for a time. There are also labyrinths on cloth that are "walked" with the finger as well as small metal labyrinths that are traced with a metal stick. A simple alternative is a labyrinth on a sheet of paper that is walked with the finger. Some Web sites contain labyrinths that can be walked using the mouse, for example the one found at www.gratefulness.org.

→ See #16 on page 210 for a labyrinth that can be enlarged and reproduced.

Veneration of Relics

A relic is something related to a saint. It can be a part of a saint's body or something that has touched the saint. The relic is kept in a special container called a reliquary and is honored by the faithful.

Prayer for the Sick

The Anointing of the Sick is a sacrament through which Jesus continues his ministry of healing. Any Catholic who is sick, elderly, or facing surgery may take advantage of the sacrament. It involves the blessing with the Oil of the Sick.

Some parishes list the sick in the church bulletin and encourage everyone to pray for them. They might even involve the sick and the homebound in a ministry of prayer for the needs of the parish.

A prayer activity that gives comfort to the sick is the making of a prayer shawl or a prayer quilt. Parishioners pray for the sick people while making the items. Together they bless the items and then they present them to the sick as reminders of their loving care.

Prayer for Enemies

Point out that the strongest way to change an enemy into

a friend is to pray for that person, perhaps because prayer changes our own attitudes. Quote Jesus' teaching about this: "But I say to you, Love your enemies and pray for those who persecute you" (Matthew 5:44).

Praying the Newspaper

The daily newspaper is filled with articles about people and situations in need of help. Suggest praying over items in the newspaper in order to encompass the whole world in prayer.

Praying Names of Jesus

Anthony De Mello, SJ, suggests giving a name to Jesus each time you inhale. Names can be drawn from Scripture or you can make up your own names: Jesus, my rock; Jesus, my life; Jesus, my joy; Jesus, my friend.

Reflections

There are a number of popular reflections—poems, allegories, and stories—that can serve as food for thought or springboards for prayer. Some of these are "One Solitary Life," "Parable of the Two Seas," "Desiderata," "Footprints," "Letter from a Friend," and "Persons Are Gifts." You might receive such reflections periodically in your e-mails from friends and acquaintances or find them on the Internet. Weave these reflections into your sessions.

STORY: *FOOTPRINTS*

One night a man had a dream. He was walking along the beach with the Lord. Across the sky flashed scenes from his life. In each scene he noticed two sets of footprints in the sand: one belonged to him, and the other to the Lord.

When the last scene of his life flashed before him, he looked back at the footprints in the sand. He noticed that many times along the path of his life there was only one set of footprints. He also noticed that it happened at the very lowest and saddest times in his life.

This really bothered him, and he questioned the Lord about it, "Lord you said that once I decided to follow you you'd walk with me all the way. But I have noticed that during the most troublesome times in my life, there was only one set of footprints. I don't understand why when I needed you most, you would leave me."

The Lord replied, "My precious, precious child, I love you and I would never leave you. During the times of trial and suffering, when you saw only one set of footprints, it was then that I carried you."

(Author unknown)

24

Resources *for Prayer*

Tons of books on prayer have been written. The collection below is of rather recent books that are linked to topics in this book. Other books, including classic books on prayer, can be found in libraries.

Bloom, Archbishop Anthony. *Beginning to Pray*. Paulist Press, 1982.

Boylan, M. Eugene. *This Tremendous Lover*. Ave Maria Press. 2009.

Camille, Alice. *The Rosary: Mysteries of Joy, Light, Sorrow and Glory*. ACTA Publications, 2003.

Canadian Conference of Catholic Bishops. *Blessings and Prayers: For Home and Family*. U.S. edition. ACTA Publications, 2008.

Chittister, Joan. *Listen with the Heart: Sacred Moments in Everyday Life*. Sheed and Ward, 2003.

Condray, Sydney. *O Gracious One: 150 Psalm-Inspired Prayers*. Twenty-Third Publications, 2005.

Costello, Gwen. *Blessed Are You! A Prayerbook for Catholics*. Twenty-Third Publications, 2005.

Duncan, Geoffrey. *600 Blessings and Prayers from Around the World*. Twenty-Third Publications, 2001.

Florian, Amy. *The Mass: An Invitation to Enjoy It*. ACTA Publications, 2003.

Glavich, Mary Kathleen, SND. *The Catholic Companion to the Psalms*. ACTA Publications, 2008.

_____. *Prayer Moments for Everyday of the Year*. Paulist Press, 2009.

Green, Thomas H., SJ. *Opening to God: A Guide to Prayer*. Ave Maria Press, 2006.

_____. *When the Well Runs Dry: Prayers Beyond the Beginning*. Ave Maria Press, 2007.

Hays, Edward. *Prayers for the Domestic Church: A Handbook for Worship in the Home*. Ave Maria Press, 2007.

_____. *Pray All Ways: A Book for Daily Worship Using All Your Senses*. Ave Maria Press, 2007.

Hutchinson, Gloria. *Praying the Rosary, Revised and Expanded*. St. Anthony Messenger Press, 2008.

Kelly, Sr. Carole Marie. *A Handful of Fire: Praying Contemplatively with Scripture*. Twenty-Third Publications, 2001.

Maloney, George, SJ. *Prayer of the Heart: The Contemplative Tradition of the Christian East*. Ave Maria Press, 2008.

Martin, James, SJ, ed. *Awake My Soul: Contemporary Catholics on Traditional Devotions*. Loyola Press, 2004.

Merill, Nan. *Psalms for Praying: An Invitation to Wholeness*. Continuum, 2006.

Nouwen, Henri. *With Open Hands*. Ave Maria Press, 2006.

Philippe, Jacques. *Time for God: A Guide to Prayer.* Pauline Books & Media, 2008.

Pope Benedict XVI. *Benedict XVI, Way of the Cross.* Pauline Books & Media, 2005.

Rupp, Joyce. *Inviting God In: Scriptural Reflections and Prayers throughout the Year.* Ave Maria Press, 2001.

Schultz, Karl A. *How to Pray with the Bible: The Ancient Prayer Form of Lectio Divina Made Simple.* Our Sunday Visitor, 2007.

Svoboda, Melannie, SND. *When the Rain Speaks: Celebrating God's Presence in Nature.* Twenty-Third Publications, 2008.

Teresa of Avila, Doheny, William, ed. *The Way of Prayer: Learning to Pray with the Our Father.* Ave Maria Press, 2008.

Thibodeaux, Mark E., SJ. *Armchair Mystic: Easing Into Contemplative Prayer.* St. Anthony Messenger Press. 2001.

CLASSIC BOOKS ON PRAYER

Introduction to the Devout Life, Francis de Sales

The Interior Castle, Teresa of Avila

The Practice of the Presence of God, Brother Lawrence

The Imitation of Christ, Thomas à Kempis

The Spiritual Exercises, Ignatius of Loyola

Trainor. Kenneth. *We Dare to Say: An Adventure in Journaling.* ACTA Publications, 2007.

Wiederkehr. Macrina. *Seven Sacred Pauses: Living Mindfully Through the Hours of the Day.* Ave Maria Press, 2008.

WEB SITES FOR PRAYER

Introduce the catechumens to Web sites that foster prayer:

The rosary www.theholyrosary.org

Stations of the Cross www.catholic.org

The Divine Office www.liturgyhours.org

Sacred Space www.jesuit.ie/prayer

The Spiritual Exercises
www.geocities.com/ourladyofthegraces

The Psalms www.praythepsalms.com

The labyrinth
www.the-peace-project.org/fingerlab.html and
www.yfc.co.uk/labyrinth/online.html

Prayers by saints www.catholicdoors.com

Sunday readings and short reflections
www.catholicnews.com/word2lif.htm

Retreat based on the Sacred Heart
www.sacredheartprayers.com

A prayer for each day of the year
prayingeachday.org

2,774 prayers
www.catholicdoors.com/prayers/index.htm

Appendix 1

Samples *and* Activities

1. Definitions of Prayer (for page 19)

Prayer is a conversation with one who we know loves us. (St. Teresa of Avila)

Prayer is wasting time gracefully.

Prayer is putting your hand in God's hand.

Prayer is a hunger.

Prayer is resting in the Lord.

In prayer we let God love us.

Prayer is joy that mounts up to God in thanksgiving. (Isaac the Syrian)

Prayer is our humble answer to the inconceivable surprise of living. (Rabbi Abraham Heschel)

Prayer is standing before God with the mind in the heart.

Prayer is enjoying the company of a Friend.

Let us leave the surface and, without leaving the world, plunge into God. (Pierre Teilhard de Chardin, SJ)

Prayer oneth the soul to God. (Julian of Norwich)

Prayer is love expressed in speech and in silence. (Catherine de Hueck Doherty)

Prayer is a twitch on the line by which God brings us home. (G.K. Chesterton)

God sits on top of our heart. When we desire to pray, the heart cracks open and God tumbles down inside. (A Hasidic explanation)

To clasp one's hands in prayer is the beginning of an uprising against the disorder of the world. (Karl Barth)

Prayer is the mortar that keeps our house together. (Blessed Teresa of Calcutta)

Prayer is when heaven and earth kiss each other. (Jewish mystic)

2. Aspirations (for page 27)

Jesus!

Jesus, Mary, Joseph!

My Lord and my God!

May the most just, most high, and most lovable will of God be done in all things done, praised, and evermore exalted.

Jesus, meek and humble of heart, make my heart like yours.

O sacrament most holy, O sacrament divine, all praise and all thanksgiving be every moment thine.

O Lord, increase our faith.

O Mary, conceived without sin, pray for us who have recourse to you.

We adore you, O Christ, and we bless you because by your holy cross you have redeemed the world.

May the Holy Trinity be blessed.

My God and my all.

May the Most Blessed Sacrament be praised and adored forever.

Send, O Lord, laborers into your harvest.

My Jesus, mercy.

Jesus, my God, I love you above all things.

O God, who are all powerful, make me a saint.

Jesus, for you I live; Jesus, for you I die; Jesus, I am yours in life and in death.

Aspirations to the Sacred Heart

Most Sacred Heart of Jesus, I place my trust in you.

O Heart of Jesus, burning with love for us, inflame our hearts with love for you.

O Heart of Jesus, all for you.

Most Sacred Heart of Jesus, have mercy on us.

O Sacred Heart of Jesus I implore that I may ever love you more and more.

3. Prayer Lab Activities (for page 29)

Station 1

Materials: A picture of Jesus.

Directions: Art is a springboard for prayer. In silence look at this picture and let Jesus speak to your heart. Respond to him as you feel moved to do.

Station 2

Materials: A few Bibles and a recording of an explanation of different reasons for praying.

Directions: Listen to the tape and then find verses from the psalms that reflect these reasons.

Station 3

Materials: Rosaries and a chart of how to pray the rosary, including a list of the four sets of mysteries.

Directions: Study the chart and memorize one set of mysteries.

Station 4

Materials: Copies of a Gospel story.

Directions: Read the story and then replay it in your mind, putting yourself in the picture. Imagine what people looked like, where they were, and their expressions. Then speak to Jesus about what happened.

Station 5

Materials: Hymnals.

Directions: Choose two hymns and analyze them. What do the words mean? What kind of prayers are they? When would you sing them?

Station 6

Materials: A list of one-line prayers such as these: Jesus; My God, I love you; My Lord and my God; My Jesus, mercy; My God and my all; Jesus, for you I live.

Directions: Choose a prayer. Sit still and repeat the prayer over and over, focusing on God dwelling in your heart.

4. Ideas for Praying in the Home (for page 60)

1. Give blessings to one another.

2. Celebrate namedays and baptismal anniversaries.

3. Pray spontaneously at special times: first driver's license, giving allowance, first date, tenth birthday, first day of school, moving into a new home.

4. Pray grace before and after meals.

5. Celebrate the Eucharist as a family. Discuss the readings before the Mass and the homily afterward. Occasionally participate in a weekday Mass together.

6. Set up a prayer corner in your home with a Bible, religious images, candles, and floral arrangements.

7. Pray the rosary together, at least a decade a day, and an entire rosary each day in May, Mary's month, and in October, the month of the rosary.

8. Attend a parish mission, retreat, or prayer service as a family.

9. Play Christian songs in the car and at home and sing along with them.

10. Visit shrines and churches other than your own.

11. Talk about prayer: the way you like to pray best, your favorite prayer, and when you pray.

12. Pray for situations in the news or in your neighborhood and for friends, relatives, and acquaintances who need help.

13. Display religious images in the house to stay mindful of God and your faith: a crucifix on bedroom walls,

pictures and statues of Jesus, Mary, and the saints, religious prayers and sayings.

14. Observe religious feasts in your home: set up a shrine for Mary in May, display blessed palm, prepare green food for St. Patrick's Day.

15. Decide what to do as a family to observe Advent and Lent, such as setting up an Advent wreath in your living room and participating in Holy Week services together.

16. Choose a patron saint for your family.

17. Make or purchase a family candle. Have it blessed and set it on your dining room table for special occasions.

18. Be creative in forming a habit of praying together at certain times, such as while driving to school or cleaning the house.

19. Memorize Scripture passages or short prayers together.

20. Designate a certain day each week as family prayer day. Take turns leading the prayer that day.

21. Begin building family prayer traditions, such as reading the nativity story together on Christmas Eve.

22. Pray a novena or a triduum to prepare for a special feast or an event such as a First Communion or a wedding.

23. Pray together on special occasions like Mother's Day, Father's Day, Thanksgiving, and birthdays.

24. Celebrate the sacrament of Reconciliation together and follow it with a special meal.

25. Write a family prayer or a family creed.

Pope John Paul II's Prayer for Families

Lord God, from you every family in heaven and on earth takes its name. Father, you are love and life. Through your Son, Jesus Christ, born of woman and through the Holy Spirit, fountain of Divine Charity, grant that each family on earth may become for each successive generation a true shrine of life and love.

Grant that your grace may guide the thoughts and actions of husbands and wives for the good of their families and of all the families in the world. Grant that the young may find in the family solid support for their human dignity and for their growth in truth and love. Grant that love, strengthened by the grace of the sacrament of marriage, may prove mightier than all the weaknesses and trials though which our families sometimes pass.

Through the intercession of the Holy Family of Nazareth, grant that the church may fruitfully carry out her worldwide mission in the family and through the family. Through Christ our Lord who is the Way, the Truth and the Life forever and ever. Amen.

5. Step Prayer (for page 68)

Take a step for love: Lord, let our love extend to our families, our friends, our neighbors, our co-workers, foreigners, and enemies, that they may be drawn closer to you.

Take a step for justice: Lord, let us work to extend your kingdom to all so that people all over the world may enjoy the basic human rights and live in peace and security.

Take a step for hope: Lord, let us go forward in confidence that you are with us and that all of your promises to us will be fulfilled.

Take a step for faith: Lord, may our belief and trust in you grow stronger so that we may witness to your loving providence.

Take a step for peace: Lord, may we be reconcilers and peacemakers in our own spheres of influence, knowing that what we do affects the whole world.

Take a step for gentleness: Lord, may we reflect your gentleness and kindness to all, especially to those most in need of love.

Take a step for patience: Lord, may we endure calmly the trials and stresses that mark our journeys through life so that they may make us better not bitter.

Take a step for courage: Lord, may we be bold in living a life of integrity, not fearing to proclaim your kingdom and to stand up for what is right and good.

Take a step for commitment: Lord, give us the grace to live our baptismal vows faithfully and to support one another so that our lives may be one grand hymn of praise to you.

6. Mass Terminology (for page 80)

Alb: long white robe the priest wears.

Altar: table on which Mass is offered; it symbolizes Christ.

Altar cloth: large cloth that covers the altar.

Ambo: lectern at which the readings are read.

Antependium: decorated material that is hung in front of the altar.

Book of the Gospels: book from which the Gospel is read at Mass; it is carried in procession.

Cassock: ankle-length robe worn by altar servers; priests sometimes wear it outside of Mass.

Chalice: cup for the wine.

Chasuble: long, sleeveless vestment the priest wears over the alb; its color matches the season of the church year or the feast.

Ciborium: lidded cup that holds the hosts.

Cincture: white rope that the priest ties around his waist over the alb.

Corporal: linen about a foot square that has a red cross in the middle of the front; the Eucharist is placed on it on the altar.

Credence table: side table in the sanctuary for articles used at Mass, such as the bread and wine, cruets, and a bowl.

Cruets: two small jars for the water and wine.

Lavabo dish: deep plate for washing the priest's fingers.

Lectionary: book of Scripture readings for Mass.

Pall: linen-covered cardboard square that covers the chalice.

Paten: plate, usually silver or gold, on which the hosts are placed.

Processional cross: cross or crucifix that leads processions.

Purificator: white cloth used to dry the priest's fingers and the vessels.

Pyx: small, round container for a sacred host outside of Mass, used to take Communion to the sick.

Sacramentary: book of prayers and directives for the Mass.

Sacristy: room where the vestments and vessels for Mass are stored.

Sanctuary: area around the altar and tabernacle.

Stole: long scarf the priest wears around his neck and over the chasuble; a deacon wears a stole over his left shoulder.

Surplice: white smock with wide sleeves worn by altar servers over a cassock; priests wear it for liturgical services other than the Eucharist.

Tabernacle: small closet that houses sacred hosts available for the sick.

7. Enthronement Ceremony: The Gift of God's Word (for page 84)

Song: A song about God's Word such as "Speak, Lord, I'm Listening"

(Process with the Bible and place it on a special stand. Let each person approach the Bible and kiss it, bow to it, or lay a hand on it and pray, "Your word, O Lord, is a lamp for my feet" (Psalm 119:105).

Leader: O good and loving God, we thank you for the gift of your word. Through Scripture you reveal yourself to us, especially in the Gospels where we meet Jesus, the Word made flesh. In Scripture you speak to us, telling us of your love for us and teaching us the way to happiness. May we always cherish your word and follow it with all our hearts.

First Reading: Isaiah 55:10–11, God's word is fruitful.

Psalm 119 (alternate sides)

> *Side 1:* Your word, O Lord, endures forever; it is as firm as the heavens. (v. 89)

Side 2: My heart stands in awe of your words. (v. 161)

Side 1: I rejoice at your word like one who finds great spoil. (v. 162)

Side 2: I trust in your word. (v. 42)

Side 1: Your word is a lamp to my feet and a light to my path. (v. 105)

Side 2: I hold back my feet from every evil way, in order to keep your word. (v. 101)

Side 1: I treasure your word in my heart (v. 11)

Side 2: I will not forget your word. (v. 16)

Side 1: I hope in your word. (v. 81)

Side 2: Be good to your servant that I may live and observe your words. (v. 17)

Side 1: The sum of your word is truth. (v. 160)

Side 2: Of your kindness, O LORD, the earth is full. (v. 64)

Reading Matthew 7:24–27 (The two houses)

Time for Reflection

Response: Lord, hear our prayer.

May we take time to listen to your word...

May we always have hearts open to your word...

May we understand your word more and more...

May we live according to your word...

May we bring others to your word...

May we always love your word...

Song A hymn of thanks and praise

8. Scripture Verses to Distribute (for page 93)

Your light must shine before others, that they may see your good deeds and give glory to your Father in heaven. *Matthew 5:16*

Whenever you pray, go to your room and shut the door, and pray to your Father who is in secret. *Matthew 6:6*

Do not store up for yourselves treasures on earth, where moth and rust consume, and where thieves break in and steal. But store up for yourselves treasures in heaven. *Matthew 6:19–20*

Do not judge, so that you may not be judged. *Matthew 7:1*

Ask, and it will be given you; search, and you will find; knock, and the door will be opened for you. *Matthew 7:7*

In everything do to others as you would have them do to you. *Matthew 7:12*

Come to me, all you that are weary, and are carrying heavy burdens, and I will give you rest. *Matthew 11:28*

If you have faith the size of a mustard seed, you will say to this mountain, "Move from here to there," and it will move; and nothing will be impossible for you. *Matthew 17:20*

Whoever wishes to be great among you must be your servant. *Matthew 20:26*

Do not fear, only believe. *Mark 5:36*

If any want to become my followers, let them deny themselves, take up their cross, and follow me. *Mark 8:34*

Be merciful, just as your Father is merciful. *Luke 6:36*

I am the resurrection and the life. Those who believe in me, even though they die, will live. *John 11:25–26*

This is my commandment, that you love one another as I have loved you. *John 15:12*

Blessed are those who have not seen and yet have come to believe. *John 20:29*

The Lord is my shepherd, I shall not want. *Psalm 23:1*

Those who seek the Lord lack no good thing. *Psalm 34:10*

Faithful friends are a sturdy shelter. Whoever finds one has found a treasure. *Sirach 6:14*

Do not fear, for I have redeemed you; I have called you by name, you are mine. *Isaiah 43:1*

When you pass through the waters, I will be with you; and through the rivers, they shall not overwhelm you. When you walk through fire you shall not be burned. *Isaiah 43:2*

All things work together for good for those who love God. *Romans 8:28*

Be steadfast, immovable, always excelling in the work of the Lord, because you know that in the Lord your labor is not in vain. *1 Corinthians 15:58*

God loves a cheerful giver. *2 Corinthians 9:7*

Be kind to one another, tenderhearted, forgiving one another as God in Christ has forgiven you. *Ephesians 4:32*

9. Scripture Verses to Match Situations (for page 93)

When I am troubled or confused	John 14:27
When I think of death	John 11:21–26
When I am in trouble	Matthew 11:28–30
When I lack confidence	Psalm 26
When someone has hurt me	Matthew 18:21–35

When I have hurt someone	Matthew 5:22–24
When I need comfort	Psalm 23, 71
When I am afraid or worried	Mark 4:31–41; Psalm 37; Psalm 73
When I want more than I have	Luke 21:1–4
When I am tempted	Psalm 55
When a friend has disappointed me	Luke 6:36–38; Psalm 41:9
When I wonder if anyone loves me	John 19:28–30; Isaiah 6:1–8; 43:1–4
When I am thankful	Psalm 38; Luke 17:11–19
When I am frightened	Luke 12:22–32; John 14:1–4; Psalm 23; Psalm 56; Psalm 91
When I need love	John 15:15; Philippians 1:7–9
When I am happy	Philippians 4:4–7; Psalm 23; Psalm 138
When I am angry	Psalm 13, Psalm 58
When it feels like God is far from me	Psalm 139
When I am discouraged	John 16:22, 33; Matthew 6:28–34; Psalm 10; Psalm 42
When I need forgiveness	Matthew 9:6–13; Mark 11:24–25; Psalm 51

When I need to forgive	Matthew 5:43–48, 6:12
When I need healing	James 5:13–16; Mark 5:35–43; Psalm 6
When I feel lonely	Psalm 71, Psalm 62
When I have deep sorrow	2 Corinthians 12:8–9; Philippians 2:13
When I feel hopeless	Mark 15:34; Psalm 13:1; Psalm 91:1, 5
When my faith is beginning to fail	Psalm 119
When I am desperate	Psalm 69:1–3, 16; Philippians 4:13
When I am exhausted	Psalm 69:1–3
When I am growing old	Psalm 71, Psalm 92
When I am the victim of injustice	Psalm 36
When I am falsely accused	Psalm 7
When people have failed me	Psalm 21
When I face a challenge	Philippians 4:13; Isaiah 6:8; Exodus 3:11–12
When I am lonely	Mark 14:37; Acts 17:28; Matthew 28:20
When I fail	Mark 15:34; Ephesians 3:20–21; 2 Corinthians 12:7

When I am exhausted	Psalm 69:1, 4;
	1 Corinthians 10:13;
	2 Corinthians 12:7
When I am envious	1 John 2:15–17;
	Hebrews 13:14;
	2 Corinthians 12:7–9
When I need God's guidance	Psalm 27:1, 14;
	Psalm 32:8;
	Ephesians 4:25–32
When I am going on a journey	Psalm 121

10. Changing Hearts of Stone (for page 94)

(Each catechumen is given a stone that represents a hard heart. A pail is placed before a crucifix.)

1. *Song* (Suggestions: "Hosea," "Jesus, Heal Us," "Remember Your Love")

2. *Prayer:* Holy Spirit, open our eyes to see how we have failed to love like Jesus. Open our hearts so that we are truly sorry for our sins for which Jesus died on the cross. Help us to make up our minds not to sin again. Strengthen our wills so that we may do penance, reject temptations, and keep from sin in the future. Fill us with such a deep love for you that we desire to please you in all our actions and words. Then our hearts will not be stony but will be like yours. We will be at peace and look forward to living forever in your kingdom. Amen.

3. *First reading:* Ezekiel 36:25–28, A Heart of Flesh

4. *Gospel reading:* The Lost Sheep (Luke 15:4–7), The Prodigal Son (Luke 15:11–32), The Sinful Woman (Luke 7:36–50), or Zacchaeus (Luke 19:1–10)

5. *Examination of conscience:* review of the Commandments

6. *Psalm* 51:1–12

7. *An Act of Contrition*

8. *Procession:* Catechumens deposit their stones in a pail before the crucifix.

9. *Song* (Suggestions: "Though the Mountains May Fall," "There's a Wideness in God's Mercy")

11. Meditation: Zacchaeus Sees Jesus (for page 110)

- Invite the catechumens to relax. Tell them they may close their eyes if they wish.

- Read the story of Zacchaeus in Luke 19:1–10.

- Retell the story, putting the catechumens into it and filling in the details.

You are in a crowd of people walking along with Jesus and the apostles. The sun is hot on your head, and the road is rocky and dusty under your feet. Everyone is excited and talking loudly. You notice Zacchaeus, the chief tax collector, in the crowd. People hate him because he works for Rome, the country that is oppressing them. Besides, Zacchaeus has become very rich because he has charged more than normal and kept the extra for himself. Now Zacchaeus is trying to see Jesus, but he is short, so he is jumping up and down in order to see over peoples' shoulders. Suddenly Zacchaeus runs ahead of the crowd and goes to a sycamore tree. He grabs the lowest branch and hoists his short, plump body up into the tree. He climbs a little higher and is half hidden among the leaves. When Jesus gets to that spot, he stops. You and the crowd all stop too.

You see Jesus peer into the tree and hear him tell Zacchaeus to come down quickly because he wants to stay at his house today. The crowd around you gasps. Zacchaeus scrambles down the tree, his face all smiles. He hugs Jesus, points the way to his house, and the two begin walking. The crowd starts making angry noises. They complain that Jesus is going to a sinner's house. Zacchaeus and Jesus stop, and you hear Zacchaeus say that he will give half of his possessions to the poor and repay fourfold to those from whom he has stolen. This is twice as much as the law requires. You see Jesus smile. He turns to the people and declares that salvation has come to Zacchaeus' house. Jesus states that he has come to seek out and save the lost.

- Lead the catechumens into reflecting on the story:

Just as Jesus seeks out Zacchaeus among the leaves, he seeks out other sinners. He seeks out us. Jesus wants us to set things right in our lives so that we will be happy. But Zacchaeus might never have been cured, if he hadn't been looking for Jesus. We too need to look for Jesus. We need to take out time in our lives to be with Jesus, to gaze upon his face, and to read about him in the Gospels. Once we've found him, we will know that he loves us and wants to be our friend. Then we can't help being like Zacchaeus and desiring to be the best person we can be. We want to stop committing sins and be worthy of Jesus' friendship. Then we will follow Jesus on the way with a light heart. This might surprise everyone, even ourselves.

- Invite the catechumens to pray:

Take a few minutes now to talk to Jesus. Tell him you want to see him.... What bad habits in your life do you know you need to change? What steps will you take to change them?… Ask Jesus to forgive you for them and to give you the grace to change.

12. Personalized Gospel Story (for page 119)

The following reflection on Luke 8:40–48 was written during a retreat after a conference on the capital sins.

Retelling of the Story

I was in the crowd hurrying after Jesus. We were noisy and jostling one another under the hot sun. We were curious to see him heal Jairus' daughter. At times Jesus was so enveloped by people I lost sight of him. Suddenly, the mob came to a standstill. Over the shoulder of the man in front of me I could see Jesus facing the crowd and searching for someone. I heard him ask, "Who touched my clothing?" One of his disciples said, "you can see how this crowd hems you in, yet you ask, 'Who touched me?'" Jesus continued to look about. Then a woman came forth trembling. She fell at his feet in fear, and we could hear her voice, breathless and shaking, as she told her story. Jesus put his hand on her head and raised her up gently. He looked into her face and said, "Daughter, it is your faith that has cured you. Go in peace and be free of this illness.

Alone with Jesus

That night walking by the Sea of Galilee with Jesus, I brought up the incident.

Conversation

"Too bad that woman had to wait so long to be cured."

"Yes," said Jesus. "If she had joined the others in the crowds to be cured, she could have been helped earlier. And the way she tried to do it—secretly—almost as if she feared I would have refused her."

"I'm like that, too, sometimes," I commented. "I run around, troubled and complaining, trying certain remedies to make myself feel better and ignore your aid. It's as if I don't apply what I say I believe. You do have power to help me. You do want to help me. You are interested in my life. Most of all, you do love me—unconditionally, as Father said last night."

"You're right," Jesus said. "I'm always ready to help you, to pick you up when you fall, to heal your wounds and hug away your hurts. Why don't you come to me?"

"Because you're invisible. I can really see you or feel your presence."

"But that doesn't mean I'm not real. Let yourself be open to the power of my love in your life, and you'll see just how real I am."

"OK. What about the sicknesses I came to see in myself during this retreat? Can you take away those pains?"

"What do you think? Don't you remember when you were learning how to drive how afraid you were each time you sat behind the wheel? You thought you'd never overcome your fear. Then all of a sudden it disappeared. You're not a hopeless case. But remember, even if you are fearful and imperfect, no matter how many capital sins you have, I still love you. Trust me. Haven't I always taken care of you?

"Yes, Lord."

13. Reflecting on the Rosary (for page 161)

St. Louis de Montfort recommended keeping focused on the mysteries by adding, after "Jesus" in the Hail Mary, words that relate Jesus to the respective mystery.

The Joyful Mysteries

Jesus incarnate
Jesus sanctifying
Jesus born in poverty
Jesus sacrificed
Jesus, Saint among saints

The Sorrowful Mysteries

Jesus in his agony
Jesus scourged
Jesus crowned with thorns
Jesus carrying his cross
Jesus crucified

The Glorious Mysteries

Jesus risen from the dead
Jesus ascending into Heaven
Jesus filling you with the Holy Spirit
Jesus raising you up
Jesus crowning you

We might add for the new Luminous Mysteries:

Jesus being baptized
Jesus performing a miracle
Jesus proclaiming good news
Jesus transfigured
Jesus giving us the Eucharist

14. Jesus' Promises to Those Who Honor His Sacred Heart (for page 172)

1. I will give them all the graces necessary for their state of life.

2. I will give peace in their families.

3. I will console them in all their troubles.

4. I will be their refuge in life and especially in death.

5. I will abundantly bless all their undertakings.

6. Sinners shall find in my Heart the source and infinite ocean of mercy.

7. Tepid souls shall become fervent.

8. Fervent souls shall rise speedily to great perfection.

9. I will bless those places wherein the image of my Sacred Heart shall be exposed and venerated.

10. I will give to priests the power to touch the most hardened hearts.

11. Persons who propagate this devotion shall have their names eternally written in my Heart.

12. In the excess of the mercy of my Heart, I promise you that my all powerful love will grant to all those who will receive Communion on the First Fridays, for nine consecutive months, the grace of final repentance: they will not die in my displeasure, nor without receiving the sacraments; and my Heart will be their secure refuge in that last hour.

15. Nine-Hour Novena to the Infant of Prague (for page 176)

This following prayer is prayed at the same time for nine consecutive hours.

O Jesus, who has said,
"Ask and you shall receive,
seek and you shall find,
knock and it shall be opened to you,"
through the intercession of Mary,

your Most Holy Mother, I knock,
I seek, I ask that my prayer be granted.
(Make your request.)

O Jesus, who has said,
"All that you ask of the Father in my name,
he will grant you," through the intercession of Mary,
your Most Holy Mother.
I humbly and urgently ask your Father
in your Name that my prayer be granted.
(Make your request.)

O Jesus, who has said,
"Heaven and earth shall pass away
but my word shall not pass,"
through the intercession of Mary,
your Most Holy Mother,
I feel confident that my prayer will be granted.
(Make your request.)

16. Labyrinth (for page 181)

Appendix 2

Catholic *Prayer* Words

adoration: our response of praise to God as we stand in awe of his great power, majesty, and goodness.

aspiration: a one-line prayer; also called *ejaculation.*

Benediction: a eucharistic devotion in which the Blessed Sacrament is exposed in a monstrance and we are blessed with it.

blessing: 1) a prayer calling on God to bestow gifts on a person or to ask God to mark a certain object or place, such as a house, with favor and divine protection; 2) can also set apart a place or object as a means of grace, for example rosaries are blessed; 3) can mean the act of God bestowing grace and favors, as when we say that God blesses us; 4) We can bless God, which means to praise God.

canticle: a sung prayer.

centering prayer: a silent prayer that focuses on God dwelling in the center of us. When attention wanders away from God, we use a word or phrase to come back to God. In essence, centering prayer is resting in God, enjoying God's presence. See *page 115*.

chaplet: a prayer form that uses beads, such as the rosary.

communal prayer: prayer that is prayed together.

contemplation: the highest form of prayer, a prayer without words. We are totally rapt in God's presence.

contrition: a prayer where we express sorrow for sin, ask forgiveness, and intend to avoid sin in the future.

Divine Office: see *Prayer of Christians*.

Eucharistic devotions: special prayers in honor of the Blessed Sacrament, such as visits to the Blessed Sacrament and Benediction.

examination of conscience: a review of our life to notice where we have cooperated with God's grace and where we haven't. It is part of preparation for the sacrament of Reconciliation and recommended to be made each night.

exposition: making the sacred host visible for adoration by setting it in a monstrance.

grace before/after meals: In grace before meals we ask God to bless us and the food we are about to eat. In grace after meals we thank God for our food.

holy hour: an hour spent in prayer usually before the Blessed Sacrament.

indulgence: the canceling of the debt of satisfaction owed for sin by certain prayers or practices. It can be partial or plenary (complete).

intention: some cause for which we offer intercessory prayer, such as world peace.

intercessory prayer: a prayer in which we ask for something on behalf of another person. Jesus is our intercessor because he constantly prays to the Father for us.

Jesus prayer: "Lord Jesus, Son of God, have mercy on me, a sinner." It is repeated over and over and can be synchronized with breathing.

journaling: writing one's thoughts and prayers, sometimes daily. This practice makes us more reflective and can produce a richer prayer life.

labyrinth: a circular path that leads to the center of a circle. As we walk the labyrinth, we pray on the way to the center, which stands for God, and on the way out into the world again.

lectio divina: sacred reading, a method of prayer that leads to union with God in contemplation. The four steps are 1) read a passage and stop when a word or phrase catches your attention; 2) reflect on your "word"; 3) respond to God in prayer; and 4) rest in the presence of God. See *page 99*.

litany: a long prayer invoking God, Mary, or a saint under many titles.

liturgy: the public worship of the Church: the Eucharist, the sacraments, and the Divine Office.

Liturgy of the Hours: see *Prayer of Christians*.

mantra: a word or phrase that is repeated continually as a prayer.

May crowning: a Marian devotion in which a statue of Mary is crowned. This usually occurs in May because it is her month.

meditation: mental prayer in which we ponder God and the mysteries of our faith.

mental prayer: prayer that occurs silently in our minds as opposed to vocal prayer, which is said out loud.

novena: praying a prayer for nine consecutive days or nine hours. The practice is derived from the nine days that Mary and the disciples prayed waiting for the Holy Spirit to come at Pentecost.

O-antiphons: nine short prayers that invoke Christ using Old Testament titles. They are prayed in the liturgy on the days right before Christmas. See *page 142.*

octave: eight days of prayer.

petition: a prayer asking God for something such as healing, a safe journey, or forgiveness. Jesus encouraged this kind of prayer.

pilgrimage: a journey to a holy place, such as the Holy Land or a shrine, for religious purposes.

prayer service: a celebration with a religious theme that incorporates Scripture, prayers, quiet time for reflection, and hymns.

procession: a religious procession is walking in honor of God usually within a liturgical or devotional service. For example, there are processions within the Mass, and on Good Friday people may process outside with a cross or statue of Christ.

Prayer of Christians: also called the Liturgy of the Hours and the Divine Office; the official daily prayer of the Church in which the entire day is sanctified. Priests and some religious are obliged to pray it, and all Christians are invited to pray it. There are seven times or hours when these prayers are prayed.

psalms: the 150 prayer-songs in the Bible's Book of Psalms. They are the Jewish prayer book, and have been adopted by

Christians. The psalms, which are Hebrew poetry, express the whole gamut of stances we have toward God: praise, lament, contrition, and thanksgiving.

Raccolta: a book that is collection of indulgenced Catholic prayers and practices. It was last published in Rome in 1898.

retreat: a period of time when we withdraw from everyday life and activities to focus on God and our relationship with God. A retreat can be a half day or as long as thirty days. Usually it has various prayer activities, including time for quiet prayer, talks by a retreat director, the celebration of the Eucharist, and the sacrament of Penance.

rosary: a Marian prayer in which we meditate on mysteries in the life of Christ while praying Our Fathers, Hail Marys, and Glory Bes on a circle of beads. Mary asked us to pray the rosary in her appearances at Lourdes and Fatima.

sacramental: a blessing or an object that has been blessed and whose use brings graces through the merits of Jesus and the prayers of the Church.

scapular: an indulgenced sacramental; two small pieces of cloth connected by strings that are worn around the neck. It shows devotion, usually to Our Lady, and is worn continually. After a person has been invested in a cloth scapular by a priest, a scapular medal may be substituted for it.

Stations of the Cross: or *Way of the Cross*; a devotion in which we remember Jesus' passion as we walk from station to station and pray. Each of the fourteen stations has a cross and art depicting one event of the passion.

spiritual bouquet: a gift of prayers and good works. It usually lists the numbers of prayer and good works that are being offered for the recipient.

spontaneous prayer: informal, vocal prayer that is not written down, prayed by rote using a formula prayer, or rehearsed.

Taizé prayer: originated with an ecumenical community of monks in Taizé, France. It mainly consists of chanting short prayers over and over alternating with periods of quiet prayer.

thanksgiving: a main purpose of prayer. We express our gratitude to God for all his loving acts of creation and redemption.

triduum: three days of prayer, such as the Holy Week Triduum of Holy Thursday, Good Friday, and Holy Saturday/Easter Sunday.

veneration of a relic: relics are parts of a saint's body, something a saint has used, or material that has been touched to a saint. These are displayed in a case called a reliquary and people may venerate, or honor, them in a ritual of prayer.

vigil light: or *votive candle*; a candle that is lit for an intention. A prayer is said and a donation is made. The flame represents the prayer rising to heaven.

vocal prayer: prayer prayed aloud.